Holistic Medicine

Holistic Medicine

Physical Health,

Peace of Mind,

and

Clarity of Consciousness

Jerry P. Gore MD

Center for Holistic Medicine
Riverwoods, Illinois

ISBN: 0976945312
ISBN 13: 9780976945314
Library of Congress Control Number: 2015909962
Center for Holistic Medicine, Riverwoods, IL

Medical Disclaimer

THE CONTENTS OF this book are intended for general information and educational purposes only. People's decisions must take into account the different circumstances and conditions unique to every individual, including but not limited to age, sex, and medical history. Only after personal consultation and examination can a doctor make a diagnosis and recommend specific treatment for you. Accordingly, this book is not intended to replace your relationship with your doctor and is not intended to be used as medical advice. Without personal consultation, the author cannot give advice about a patient or a particular medical condition. Individuals should always see a competent health-care provider before using any suggestions in this book. Names and other details in the case histories have been changed to alter the identities of the patients. Any use of the material discussed in the following pages is at the reader's own discretion and is the reader's sole responsibility.

Dedication

I AM DIVINELY BLESSED to have my wife, Carol, who is my soul mate. I could not have written this book without her support. I would also like to thank my loving sons, Ariel, Aaron, and Daniel, who indeed served as "subject matter" for much of the information in this book; my mother, Beverly Gore and mother- in- law, Irene Goren, whose generosity of spirit and wisdom continue to inspire us all; my father, Morrie Gore of blessed memory whom I am sure helped our Center from above since the first day of its inception; my father-in-law, Marvin Goren, MD of blessed memory who lovingly "had my back" during my early years in holistic medicine; my wonderful patients and teachers, especially my esteemed teacher Rudolph Ballentine, MD and beloved Rabbi Daniel Moscowitz of blessed memory; my experience at the Himalayan Institute in Glenview, Illinois; and my colleagues and friends, including Larry Cohen, MD, and Dennis Chernin, MD, who were always there when I needed them.

Contents

Preface

I BELIEVE THAT it is possible to achieve physical health, peace of mind, and clarity of consciousness using holistic medicine.

Physical health refers to our body. We deserve to have a body that can support a lifestyle of movement, productivity, and mental and emotional growth and that becomes a suitable receptacle for the soul housed within it.

Peace of mind refers to our emotional/intellectual psyche. Our mind needs to drop the old reflexive and dysfunctional behavior patterns that tie us down and bind us to the past, not allowing us to be fully present in the moment with all our adult capabilities. Our mind also needs to learn and continually provide us with an uplifting and comforting perspective on life, so we can relax and enjoy the adventure of life as we grow in an upward direction.

Clarity of consciousness refers to a partnership between our body, mind, and spirit. I think of this clarity as our ability to be conscious of something higher while simultaneously living in the physical everyday world of work, family, and recreation. This state of consciousness is an achievement we can obtain and affords us the ability to feel our soul within us as we live in a very demanding world. With physical health, peace of mind, and clarity of consciousness, we have the tools to change ourselves in a positive way, fulfill our potential for which we were created, and, at the same time, help the world around us to become a better place.

Introduction

Early Difficulties

In the late '70s and early '80s, I encountered great personal and professional difficulty. I had good intentions and some skills and training. I was armed with a basic medical education from a fine medical school and had postgraduate training from a prestigious university in classical psychiatry as well as a supplemental program in humanistic psychology, yet something went wrong. I felt unfulfilled professionally, and my actions were causing pain and suffering in those around me. I did not want to experience the twenty-four-hour day as split up between good and bad. I finally decided that I would no longer continue my life without a deeper sense of satisfaction and meaning both personally and professionally, and I began to pray for guidance and direction.

New Directions

I looked into various traditions from the East, such as yoga, aikido, and tai chi. I began to study with teachers who embraced a concept of the wholeness (body, energy, mind, and spirit) of a person. This included the study of nutrition and supplementation as it applied to illness and wellness, and I began experimenting with my diet. I studied homeopathy as a natural medical system that could be applied to symptoms as well as to prevention and wellness, and I began using them for my patients and myself. I became a student of yoga philosophy and looked deeper into my personal upbringing, including the roots of my own religion.

These traditions and teachings really opened my eyes to the world around me. They spoke of a subtle reality unfolding from the inside. Imagine consciousness being the ground of existence; from this emerges the psychological, in turn birthing the energy fields we live in and finally ending in the manifestation of the physical world we take for granted.

I began to incorporate a daily practice of stretching (hatha-yoga), breathing, meditation, learning, and prayer. What followed in the way of teachers, teachings, and experiences became the foundation for a new life—one in which the practice of medicine and living life became a twenty-four-hour opportunity for changing myself and helping others as I sought my true destiny. Over time, I experienced a deep sense of fulfillment and completion as a doctor. The divine blessed me so that I was allowed to doctor the physical, energetic, and mental aspects of my patients and myself as well as helping them connect within and find meaning in their personal and work lives.

As I connected to my own soul personally and professionally, it seemed that the bouquet of my life flowered out as I witnessed the poetry and miracles associated with this transformative and deeply curative medicine we call holistic medicine.

Overview

First, I want to address the need for a more holistic way of approaching medicine.

Second, I want to share with you some useful body/mind perspectives I have learned to help me think about how to approach symptoms. I will refer to them as "basic concepts," and wherever possible, I endeavor to include relevant case examples to make the concepts clear and practical.

Third, I believe that using holistic medical techniques and theory, we can achieve physical health, peace of mind, and clarity of consciousness.

Physical Health

I believe we deserve a body that can support a lifestyle of movement, physical productivity, and mental and spiritual growth. In order to accomplish this, I offer some ideas on food for health as well as some thoughts about herbal medicine with some examples of the use of herbs. I then proceed to discuss some traditional and nontraditional ideas concerning exercise and health.

I then go on to discuss "energy medicine" because I consider the "energy body" as a transitional zone between the body and the mind, and I experience energy medicine as very healing with few side effects.

Peace of Mind

I offer two methods. First is an intimate look at psychotherapy as a tool for the removal of that special kind of conflict that ties us down and anchors us to the past with old reflexive, dysfunctional behavior patterns that we repeat with present relationships. The second method I offer is a philosophical and spiritual perspective involving "divine providence," the need for an individual soul correction, and the need to contribute and help the world. This approach provides us with an uplifting and comforting perspective on life so we can relax and enjoy the adventure of life with a more steady internal state.

Clarity of Consciousness

With peace of mind, we are freed up to climb the ladder of consciousness and to fly without wings, so to speak. How can we do this? We cultivate the ability to turn inward, connect to our soul within, and change for the better. We also turn outward and strive to fulfill our self-expression through helping a world correction take place around us. To do this, I discuss tools such as breathing techniques and a yogic model of the mind to help us understand our objectives. I then go on to discuss a bit of the theory and practice of the art of meditation that I consider practical and fulfilling.

Then I pull all this together in "a day in the life" and suggest a twenty-four-hour action plan for health, followed by a little poetry of holistic medicine as expressed through three true case histories.

Part One

Basic Concepts

THESE BASIC CONCEPTS that I will share with you have provided me with the opportunity as a physician to reach specific goals both in patient care and for my own health in the areas of physical health, peace of mind, and clarity of consciousness. I attempt to clarify these concepts by including relevant case examples to make the information clear and practical.

In chapter 1, I ask and answer the question, why do we need holistic medicine? In chapter 2, I need to demonstrate the large and empowering context that holistic medicine affords the doctor in treating patients and also describe the many possibilities for cure. I do this by bringing a working definition of holistic medicine by presenting a dialogue with a patient diagnosed with asthma. In chapter 3, I discuss the philosophy of "sheaths of functioning" with case examples. Chapter 4 briefly describes many holistic techniques and therapies under the heading "Tools for Life" that can be used in the various sheaths or functional levels. Additionally, in chapter 5, I explain another perspective called "yoga-chakra theory of medicine." The final basic concept I discuss in chapter 6 concerns the subject of Ayurvedic medicine.

1

Why We Need Holistic Medicine

Holistic Medicine versus Traditional Medicine

HOLISTIC MEDICINE TAKES into account the body, energy, mind, and spirit of the patient. Conventional medicine is focused on the body. I will elucidate this idea as we proceed further.

Patient Education

Holistic Medicine Encourages Learning about Your Illness

Holistic medicine prefers to educate the patient about his or her health. This usually results in growth and self-empowerment of the "sick" person as he or she progresses from helpless and uninformed patient to become a student of his or her own health.

Doctor Becomes Educator, and Patient Becomes Student

For example, in a case of asthma, instead of medicating away the shortness of breath, the patient with asthma may use this symptom as an opportunity to learn about himself or herself as follows:

- Decrease Mucus-Producing Foods
  Learn that certain foods are known to produce mucus in everyone, which makes breathing more difficult in the asthmatic. Did you know that bananas stimulate the body to make mucus, whereas apples (especially green) decrease bodily mucus? Therefore, it is therapeutic to avoid mucus-producing food and consume those foods that reduce mucus.
- Relax the Windpipe
  Supplements such as magnesium help smooth-muscle tissue surrounding the bronchial tubes relax, resulting in less constriction and wider airways. This effect results in breathing more easily. Therefore, let's add a supplement recommendation for magnesium and note that we are beginning to create a treatment plan that at this point is based on education concerning food and supplements.
- Reduce Inflammation
  Fish oils EPA (eicosapentaenoic acid) and DHA (docosahexaenoic acid) may help decrease inflammation, which helps reverse the pathology of asthma. Add this to the plan.
- Breathe Easier
  Next, teach that person a more efficient way to breathe. We call this diaphragmatic breathing. Anyone, especially children, can learn how to do it. Watch how the anxiety that goes

with struggling to breathe goes down as the person's breathing awareness goes up.

- Utilize Energy Medicine
  Now let's move on to energy medicine. In my experience, homeopathy or acupuncture can greatly reduce or remove altogether the vulnerability to asthma. This is a deeper level of cure, because when energy medicine is used, the person's own body and immune system have changed for the better. This concept will be explained more fully in chapter 12 on energy medicine and chapter 13 on homeopathic medicine.
- Address Stress
  Finally, we must inquire if this person is under stress. Is there an emotional component to his or her history? Is he or she living in the middle of a family difficulty? If so, then the symptoms of asthma may be a cry for help from the person's body and/or mind, and he or she needs to be listened to. When the emotional issue is articulated, the person can now work on improving it, changing it, and observing how this positive change helps "lighten the load" on the lungs.

Interactive Treatment Plan

We took the example of asthma and showed how to create a treatment plan involving education, personal accountability, and self-empowerment. It looks like this: stop mucus-producing foods, take magnesium for bronchodilation, take fish oils or consume cold-water fish for an anti-inflammatory effect, learn to breathe diaphragmatically, and work with stress or emotional difficulties so they do not "somatize" into bodily symptoms.

Your Illness Is Your Ticket to Learning

The idea here is that your symptoms or illness become your own unique opportunity for learning and growth—your own personal university curriculum, if you will—and not necessarily just something to suppress, cut out, or get rid of. But you may wonder, why not just take some medication, obtain relief, and get on with life? Why has nature bothered to give us "dis-ease" to learn from? What is the reason behind this? The answer, I believe, is that our body/mind is like everything else in this amazing world around us—constantly whispering the daily message, "Grow as a human being."

Traditional Medicine Focuses on Symptom Relief

Conventional medicine focuses on symptom relief. I want to explain this concept a little more fully. Modern medicine is very good at treating a symptom by trying to reverse its effects or removing it. This can be lifesaving, as in an episode of appendicitis or during a life-threatening asthma attack or acute infection. However, many symptoms are not life threatening but are signs that something in the human body/mind is amiss (dis-ease) and needs rebalancing. Should this be the case, many people with these symptoms can benefit from a perspective on health and healing that provides self-discovery, growth, and empowerment.

Evolution and Growth

How can a medical plan empower a person? Simple. Teach someone how to help him- or herself, and watch how that person's curiosity and sense of experimentation grow. Something "clicks" inside them as they sense they have power over their own health destiny.

Holistic Medicine Encourages the Evolution of Patient to Student to Teacher

In the above example of the person with asthma, she was surprised to learn that foods could affect her condition and that certain foods actually increased mucus in her airways! No conventional doctor had ever said that before. She stopped those foods! She was equally surprised to learn breathing techniques that she could practice on her own. She practiced focusing on her breathing daily. She began as an unknowing "patient." As her curiosity and enthusiasm took hold, she became a "student" of her condition and experimented with foods and practiced diaphragmatic breathing. She not only felt better but felt like she grew as a person, obtaining a little bit of self-actualization using her medical condition as the vehicle for her personal learning and growth. Others noticed her sense of confidence and growing mastery over her health. They began asking her for her advice, and she was glad to share her knowledge, thus completing the trilogy of evolutionary steps we see so often.

Someone begins as a patient, evolves to a student, and then becomes a teacher to others: patient to student to teacher. This is the wonderfulness of holistic medicine because it views these symptoms as opportunities for learning and growth. Grow through your asthma. Grow through your arthritis. Grow through your anxiety. Learn and educate yourself. Approaching medicine this way offers an opportunity to learn from your personal health circumstances whatever they may be and is consistent with the idea that we humans are here to grow.

Traditional Medicine Encourages Reliance on Medication

Contrast this to your experience in conventional medicine. The patient has a symptom diagnosed as asthma. In an emergency, this traditional medicine can be lifesaving. However, as mentioned above, the majority of situations are not emergencies. Often, the following scenario takes place. A person visits his or her doctor, who prescribes a bronchodilator with instructions on how to take the medicine, and both doctor and patient look for symptom relief. As time goes on, in the absence of education or the kind of growth described above, patients develop the expectation to just stay on the medicine or stop taking the medicine one day and hope for the best.

Effect on Immune System

Holistic Medicine Strengthens

This is an important concept. If you have an infection and are given an antibiotic, it may kill the germ, but how have you changed? The symptoms of fever or pain may be gone, but has your immune system strengthened or weakened? In holistic medicine, the nutrition, supplementation, or energy medicine strengthens your immunity, and then something miraculous takes place. Your immune system "kicks out" the bug, virus, or parasite or heals the inflammation. The healing power is in you, and it's you who ends up stronger after that bout of illness than before. Think about this. Challenges in life are meant to make us stronger, not weaker. This is what nature desires—that we overcome a medical challenge and become stronger as a result.

Traditional Medicine May Weaken

In contrast, if you use conventional medicine, what does it accomplish? It may remove your symptoms; however, your immunity is the same or even weaker than before because you removed the pathogen with an external medicine rather than your immune system driving it out. In addition, there may be some side effects from the medication that weakens your system, and your vulnerability to the original infection has not improved and may even have increased!

Safety

Holistic Medicine Is Generally Safe

In my years of experience, I have seen that the use of foods, herbs, vitamins, homeopathic remedies, and stress-reduction techniques can be applied to a broad range of people from infancy through the elderly years and across cultures and nationalities with hopes for helping people, and when carefully prescribed and monitored, these therapies produce few worries about side effects.

Conventional Medicine Is Very Strong

As you know, modern laboratory medicines are very potent, have the potential to cause harm, and must be closely monitored in all situations. We rarely see such difficulties when using holistic therapies because, in my opinion, side effects are few, are easily monitored, and are rarely severe.

Cost-Effectiveness

Holistic Medicine Is Cost-Effective

Recently, I treated a young lady for a left-sided sore throat. I recommended some vitamins, an herb, and a homeopathic remedy. The vitamin cost $12, the herb cost $9.50, and the remedy cost $8. They could all be used many times over.

Conventional Medicine Is Costly

At this date, commonly used antibiotics may cost $30 to $40 for a one-time course of treatment. Prescription medicine may be very costly.

A Word of Caution

I value conventional medicine for its potential to save lives in serious situations, and I encourage many patients not to drop their medications suddenly without supervision of a competent health practitioner. For some people with serious problems, it may take time to learn lifestyle changes, and it may be best for them to experiment with conventional medicine and a holistic program that works for them simultaneously. This should be an enjoyable learning process that proceeds in a timely and safe manner. With that in mind and for all the reasons I mentioned above, I feel quite comfortable using and recommending holistic medicine for many of the issues we see in general practice day to day.

Next, I want to explore the ideas that help me create a holistic treatment plan for people with medical issues or formulate a wellness plan for those who want to live more healthfully. Let's proceed by first defining holistic medicine.

2

Defining Holistic Medicine—Using the Example of Asthma

I THINK OF holistic medicine as both a philosophy and a technique.

Philosophy

I view a person's symptoms or condition of illness as something to learn and grow from. They are very personal to each of us, are not random, and usually represent an imbalance in our life that needs correcting. If we use the symptom of an illness to learn more about ourselves, we feel more in control and more self-empowered. Then illness isn't so scary or so foreign, we do not feel like a victim to something we don't understand, and we are less dependent on others to "fix" us with medications or surgery, which often try to stop the symptoms without really getting to the cause, and getting to the cause would be curative.

Techniques

Any form of medical therapy can be used as right action at the right time in a person's life as his or her next growth step. Years ago, I felt that we should use techniques that were basically educational in nature so that each person could learn and take complete control over his or her illness and wellness. Over time, I have utilized a whole array of helpful approaches such as nutrition (foods and supplements), body therapies (massage, naprapathy, myofascial release therapy), energy therapies (homeopathy, acupuncture, breathing), psychological therapies (psychotherapy, energy therapy, counseling, hypnosis), and practical spiritual interventions (prayer, contemplation, meditation) including searching for his or her unique purpose in life.

Revisiting Asthma with a Hypothetical Conversation

Jodie, a thirty-six-year-old computer programmer and mother of two, complained, "I'm tired of these bronchodilators, which make me feel wired, and I'm depressed over always feeling a tightness in my chest when it's cold or when I exercise or when I visit someone with a cat. Besides, I feel like a victim—a victim to weather, to activity, to animals, etc. Is there anything I can do to help myself?"

First Approach: Nutrition

I told her, "Yes, there is. There is an Ayurvedic concept that certain foods increase mucus in the airways. These foods create problems in other conditions as well, such as bronchitis, sinusitis, and allergies.

Stop taking wheat, dairy, and bananas, for starters. Live foods, such as fresh, raw fruits and veggies, are preferred over frozen or canned. This alone should help a lot. Besides this, add a natural anti-inflammatory such as fish oil and a natural bronchodilator such as magnesium. You'll feel better."

Jodie was surprised with the idea that food could affect her symptoms and said, "This is something that I could really try." She wondered why no one had ever discussed this with her before.

Second Approach: Energy Medicine

"Jodie, there is another way," I continued. "Try energy medicine such as homeopathy or acupuncture. Homeopathy is the science of medical therapeutics where we use very dilute portions of plants, minerals, or animal tissues and individualize this treatment for you.

For instance, your asthma might be worse from exercise, cold air, and tobacco smoke; if so, try Lobelia (from the Indian tobacco plant), and after a few doses, you might find yourself very much improved. But if your friend has asthma that is made worse during dampness, he could take Natrum Sulphuricum. If his asthma is worse after indigestion, he would take Nux Vomica! You see, three people have asthma but require three different remedies because homeopathy looks for the symptoms unique to that individual instead of treating everyone with asthma with the same medicine. I repeat—we are looking to find out how the asthma expresses itself uniquely in that individual, and we use that uniqueness to find a specific treatment that fits that person instead of one-remedy-fits-all asthma." Jodie marveled at the thought of a medicine tailored to her specific symptoms.

Third Approach: Breathing-Technique Education

"I would like to describe something else worth trying. Let's examine your breathing. Put one hand on your chest and one hand on your tummy. Which hand moves while you breathe?"

"My hand on my chest does," she said.

I answered, "Did you know that chest breathing tends to stimulate the fight-or-flight response in our body and creates anxiety? Try a more efficient method of breathing called 'diaphragmatic breathing.' In the first stage of breathing, watch how the belly moves outward during inhalation and inward during exhalation. Keep the movement equal and smooth. The second stage involves the lateral expansion of the ribs on either side. Feel all that air filling up from bottom to top."

Jodie became relaxed. Her whole demeanor changed as she focused on her breathing. Gradually gaining in confidence and feeling more relaxed, she said, "Tell me more!"

Fourth Approach: Cleansing

"Yes, Jodie, I'll tell you more. The topic here is cleansing, which is sadly neglected in the West. Did you know you could buy a little teapot-like structure called a 'neti pot,' fill it with water and a few pinches of sea salt, and pour the water through your nose? This clears out mucus, opens clogged sinuses, and leaves you with the feeling of 'I can breathe through my nose.' Other more advanced washes exist so that a person can literally wash out mucus from the stomach that accumulated overnight. This washing effect really helps me breathe much easier. Some people also do this in the change of seasons as a preventive."

"Really?" Jodie said, sounding less and less like a victim. "Anything else?"

Fifth Approach: Emotions

"Yes, Jodie. There is another concept I want to share with you. Yoga theory would say that the symptom of asthma involves the heart chakra, which affects the expression of love, nourishment, and relationship with others. It's inspiring to see a person use his or her difficulty expressing air (asthma) as a metaphor to examine his or her feelings, thoughts, hopes, and conflicts involving love and relationships. Indeed, the very symptom of the illness becomes the individual's opportunity to grow and learn about himself or herself in a new and powerful way."

What followed was a brief conversation about some of the stresses in her life and how they were affecting her. You would think that bringing these things up would upset her more, but we observed the opposite. Her sharing with another human being brought about a noticeable relaxation. Even her face looked more relaxed.

At this point, Jodie had a doctor's bag full of nutrition, supplements, homeopathic remedies, breathing techniques, and cleansing techniques. She also had an idea about where to take her next emotional step. Looking confident and solid with her newfound skills and knowledge, she turned to me and said, "Yes, Dr. Gore, there is another way."

3

Sheaths of Life

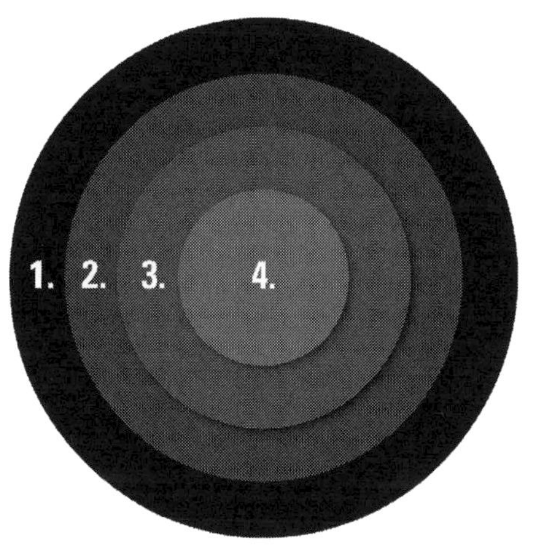

1. PHYSICAL SHEATH:
LOCATION: THE BODY
i.e. cells, tissues, and organs

2. ENERGY SHEATH:
LOCATION: MERIDIANS/NADIS
Energy pathways can be unbalanced or blocked, resulting in physical/emotional problems.

3. MENTAL SHEATH:
LOCATION: MIND/CONSCIOUS & UNCONSCIOUS
Conflicts, worries, stresses will affect the energy pathways and physical body.

4. WISDOM SHEATH:
LOCATION: REALM OUTSIDE OF TIME AND SPACE
Using this information to help answer questions such as work fulfillment, purpose in life, rewarding relationships, time-related transitions, one's true destiny and how they affect your health.

Figure 3-1. The four sheaths of life.

The Sheaths of Life

An Indian philosophy known as *Sankhya* teaches that a human being is made up of coordinated levels of functioning called *koshas*. "*Kosha*" means "sheath" and I will use the terms "sheath" and "level" interchangeably in this book. (See figure 3-1.) There are many sheaths and I will discuss four sheaths that I use in my work as follows:

1. *The physical or food sheath* is the physical body, consisting of its cells, tissues, organs, and organ systems, and is the most external sheath.
2. *The energy sheath* consists of the expansive network of energetic pathways (referred to as *meridians* in traditional Chinese medicine and *nadis*, Sanskrit for "tube" in traditional Indian medicine), which provide pathways for the energy to travel throughout the physical body. This level is subtle to the food sheath and is said to connect the body to the mind.
3. *The mental sheath* consists of the conscious and unconscious mental functioning including access to present and past memories, sense impressions from all our senses, and the reservoir of all our experiences recorded in our consciousness.
4. *The wisdom sheath* is that part of us that literally resides outside the mind/body in the realm of the spirit.

These levels are interconnected and work together to form the whole person. This expansive view of how a person functions allows the physician to see the greater picture and to creatively move to the sheath or combination of sheaths likely to help you with your specific problem or wellness quest. In other words, we can make a diagnosis of imbalance in a particular level and then choose a technique or remedy or educational tool that fits that specific level. This affords the holistic doctor great depth and breadth in diagnosis and treatment. I will briefly discuss the sheaths with case examples.

Food Sheath (*Annamaya Kosha*)

This level of functioning represents the physical body—quite literally with all its cells, organs, organ systems, and body parts. Food and exercise play a major role in its functioning. There are many tools to help here, as most allopathic/conventional medicine and many alternative medicine techniques are focused here.

(See figure 4-1 in chapter 4.)

Case Example: Physical Intervention Relieves a Physical Symptom

Cathy is five years old, and her mom is worried because Cathy has had repeated ear infections. Her doctor is suggesting she have tubes surgically placed in her ears to help drain the fluid that accumulates in her ear canals. This fluid can be a home for bacteria to grow in her ear. Repeated doses of antibiotics have not been able to keep the infections away. Similar to Jody's asthma (discussed in chapter 2), we were able to recommend a diet that reduced the mucus production in her ears (less dairy, wheat, and sugar). We also added some vitamins and fish oil rich in anti-inflammatory EPA and DHA. In a few months, her symptoms cleared up completely without antibiotics, and she avoided the necessity of surgery. This is an example of the problem occurring in the physical sheath (the middle ear) and the tools to help (diet and supplements) coming from the physical level of intervention. (See figure 4-1 in chapter 4.)

Energy Sheath (*Pranamaya Kosha*)

This level of human functioning refers to the energy part of our bodies. In Western medicine, this concept is generally not acknowledged and therefore not used by most physicians. In the East, this energy is known variably as *prana* in India, *chi* in China, and *ki* in Japan and Asia. Energy is said to flow through energy channels that energize our tissues and organs. In traditional Chinese medicine, the physician uses needles (acupuncture) or finger pressure (acupressure) applied to specific points in the body to make sure the *chi* is flowing properly through the energy channels, the meridians, because too little or too much energy creates disease in the physical body. In yoga, the student is taught breathing exercises to help the *prana* move through the thousands of energy channels, the *nadis*. In China, millions of people use tai chi exercise to maintain wellness, by keeping the flow of *chi* in balance.

Another popular energy medicine is homeopathy. Homeopathy is a form of medical therapeutics whereby the essence of a plant, mineral, or animal tissue is extracted from the material, and its energy is given to a person to fit the symptoms of the case (see chapter 13 on homeopathy). It's considered an energy medicine because in the making of the homeopathic remedy, the dilution process eliminates most, if not all, of the molecules of the original plant or mineral, leaving behind the energy of the substance to perform the healing action, hence the term "energy medicine."

Case Example: Energy Medicine Helps Relieve a Physical Symptom

I received a phone call from a clergyman desperate to help his wife. She had broken her arm and was in pain unrelieved by traditional pain-killers (pain medication is a physical sheath intervention). She couldn't sleep or cook, and the family of eight children and husband were in difficult straits. I recommended homeopathic Arnica (from the plant Arnica Montoya) to be taken four to six times a day (an energy-sheath intervention). That very day, she experienced relief and slept through the night. After a few days, she reported no longer having pain, much to the family and husband's relief.

This demonstrates an example of successfully treating a physical symptom (pain) with an energetic healing modality (Arnica). Acupuncture is often used as a treatment for pain and would be another example of an energy treatment applied to a physical symptom.

Mental Sheath (*Manomaya Kosha*)

The mental sheath includes the history of our conscious and unconscious thoughts, feelings, perceptions, and memories. It includes the experiences of our sensory impressions recorded in our brain and body, such as what we think, feel, see, smell, touch, and taste. For this reason, it is important to screen out what you do not want in your mind, such as the tragic news on the daily newspaper's front page, just as you would not hesitate to screen out a piece of rotten food from your meal. In my training at the Himalayan Institute, we were taught to think of the mind's functions as illustrated in the following diagram. (See figure 3-2.)

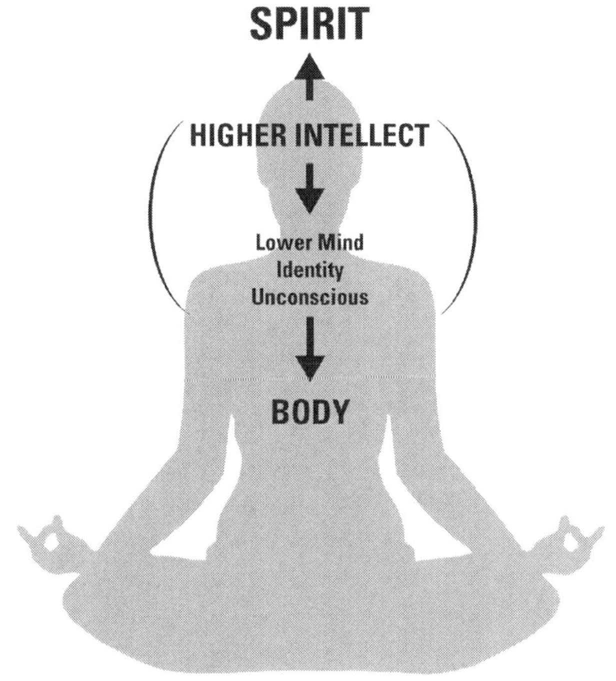

Figure 3-2. The yoga model of the mind.

1. The higher intellect (*buddhi*) is the witness part of the mind that is able to decide, discriminate, discern, and bring the matter to truth. It is also the part of the mind that is capable of connecting to that experience that is considered to be outside the mind, i.e., the spiritual world. This is demonstrated in the illustration by showing an arrow connecting the higher intellect to the other parts of the mind and at the same time, another arrow connecting it to the realm of the spirit. Its function is to become a vessel for spiritual information to flow into the mind and to coordinate optimal mental functioning between all parts of the mind.

2. The lower mind (*manas)* is responsible for "lower," more reflexive thinking, including doubt, and recording perception of the five senses.
3. Identity (*ahamkara*) is the part of the mind where we feel that cohesive sense of "I am-ness" or "This is who I am," i.e., "I am a man," "I am pretty," or "I am good/no good."
4. The unconscious (*chitta*), called "the memory banks of the mind," is where all impressions in this life (and any past lives) are stored.

Case Example: The Mind Affects a Urinary-Tract Infection

I had the pleasure of treating a twenty-eight-year-old professional woman who suffered from chronic, recurrent cystitis—in plain language, painful urinary-tract infections. After trials of antibiotics that worked only temporarily, she desired to try holistic medicine. At first, we intervened with the physical sheath by working with her diet. She gave up her sugary ways and also lightened up on the heavy, greasy meals fried in vegetable oils. We added a simple multivitamin and a probiotic to reintroduce the good bacteria into her gut that were destroyed by the antibiotics. She improved and felt better, too. However, the progress did not hold, and her symptoms returned.

Next, we turned to the energy sheath and tried some homeopathic remedies that have helped many women experiencing similar symptoms. Cantharis was one of the remedies we utilized. Again, she improved for a while but returned with the symptoms in full force.

We then moved to the mental sheath and began questioning her stress levels and emotional life. I knew that very often cystitis is related to anger that is not expressed and is held within (hence the expression "pissed off!"). After some discussion, she admitted that she had been very angry with her husband for a very long time. She had tried many ways to work out things with him and had been unsuccessful. I listened compassionately and suggested some counseling might be useful, but in her case, she was not open to that method at that time. I cared about her, and I wondered how she was going to solve this problem, as her mind was affecting her body so dramatically, and the cure seemed to be to improve her marriage in some way that seemed impossible at that time.

Time went by, and I didn't see her for a while. Then, after several months, much to my surprise, she came in one day and announced, "I no longer have urinary-tract infections anymore!"

"What did you do?" I asked.

She calmly reported that she had divorced her husband, was no longer angry, was living in her own apartment, and felt that she would no longer have a problem. Wow. This is a very dramatic example of how the mind was affecting the body and how a mindful intervention (and indeed a lifestyle intervention) brought about a cure. I have encountered many people who were able to cure their physical symptoms after using psychotherapy or other forms of counseling. In some instances, energy remedies are capable of reaching into the mental sheath and working with it to bring relief. In the above case, I believe marital counseling could have been effective in improving her marriage and removing her chronic cystitis, but in the end, she chose to have a lifestyle change that worked for her.

Wisdom Sheath (*Vijnanamaya Kosha*)

The Spiritual Part of Ourselves

According to Sankhya philosophy, there are levels of spiritually. This level connects us directly to the spiritual part of ourselves, from where intuition and creativity flow. Do not confuse this with the thoughts and feelings that come from our logical mind or our unconscious. Intuition comes from beyond the body/mind, beyond the space-time continuum. In kabala, this is known as knowledge—the flash of insight (*chochma*). How do we gain access to this magnificent aspect of ourselves?

We have all had the experience at some time in our lives of information coming to us while we are relaxing in a shower, running on a beach, or engaging in a mindless activity that frees the mind to be open to information that comes from outside ourselves. On the other hand, we can deliberately train our mind in the use of prayer to rise above ourselves, or to meditate and free the mind, empty it of thoughts, and become an observer to the flow of consciousness as described in the chapter on meditation (chapter 19). Physical health, peace of mind, and clarity of consciousness then partner with divinity.

As a doctor, I use the sheaths as a systematic diagnostic tool. As in the above examples, a health practitioner can use the perspective of the sheath that will yield the most results to help a patient's symptoms or to create a plan for wellness, and the sheaths give me tremendous latitude for doing this. To have physical health, peace of mind, and clarity of consciousness, it is helpful to first correct, nourish, and strengthen the physical, energetic, and mental sheaths. This allows the spiritual realm to open up like a flower sharing its aroma. We can then develop the tools necessary to sense that bouquet and partner with the divine on a regular basis.

4

Tools for Life: Matching Healing Modalities to Their Appropriate Level

WHOLE HEALTH DIAGRAM

1. PHYSICAL LEVEL:

Dietary & Nutritional Therapy
Vitamins & Supplements
Ayurvedic Techniques
Cleansing Techniques
Herbal Therapy
Chiropractic
Massage Therapy
Feldenkrais®
Yoga & Exercise

2. ENERGY LEVEL:

Breathing Exercises
Therapeutic Touch
Relaxation Techniques
Acupuncture
Acupressure
Homeopathy
Flower Essences

3. MENTAL LEVEL:

Yoga Chakra Therapy
Psychotherapy/Counseling
Journaling

4. SPIRITUAL LEVEL:

Meditation
Contemplation
Prayer

Figure 4-1. The whole health diagram of tools for life.

PREVIOUSLY, WE DISCUSSED a yoga philosophy, describing various sheaths or levels, their application in the practice of holistic medicine, and some case examples. Now I want to discuss techniques one may use as tools and organize them according to the functional levels. (See figure 4-1.)

As all levels are interconnected, the tools designated to affect a particular level indirectly affect the other levels as well. Take nutrition, for example. The correct diet for you not only makes you feel physically good but also has an effect on your energy, mental state, and spiritual clarity. The basic principle and amazing health opportunity I want you to grasp is that a specific medical technique or knowledge, although usually seen as mainly affecting a specific sheath of functioning, may affect all the other areas of functioning as well. All the tools that affect their appropriate sheaths of functioning are at your disposal. Be ready to use them anytime in any case to help a person or to help yourself. If you learn a new technique, just classify it into the physical, energetic, mental, or spiritual part of your toolbox. Please take note. The discussion below is not intended to be a detailed or all-inclusive review of available therapeutic techniques.

Expand Your Creativity as a Healer

My goal here is to introduce you to the use of these medical tools and how they relate to the notion of different sheaths of functioning. This is an expanded way of thinking about diagnosis, treatment, and wellness, and I want to share with you the excitement of being a healer and promoting wellness when all these possibilities are at your disposal.

Physical Level—the Body

Diet and Nutrition

Food is the most common and easily identified area of medical therapeutics that affects our physical, energetic, emotional, and even our spiritual state (try meditating after eating a burger, fries, and a shake—just kidding). That is why the physical sheath is called the *annamaya kosha*; in Sanskrit, *annamaya* means food. Our bodies reflect our food choices. Why are there so many diets and food strategies such as vegetarian, vegan, low-carbohydrate/high fat and protein, gluten-free, raw, high fiber, and macrobiotic, just to name a few? This is because what you eat really makes a difference, and not only that, food affects each of us differently. After many years of lecturing about different aspects of nutrition that I felt strongly about, people were asking me, "Where can I read about this stuff?" I have included this information in the section on physical health, in chapters 7, 8, and 9.

Vitamins and Supplements

This is a booming industry because supplements can make a difference and are fairly easy to conceptualize as a physical tool that affects both the body and the mind. A few examples follow.

Calcium, boron, vitamin D, magnesium, and other minerals are commonly recommended to strengthen bone. Magnesium is a wonderful muscle relaxant that is used in a variety of clinical situations including asthma, muscle cramping, and in antianxiety formulations. B_6 and magnesium can help the painful cramping and mood changes associated with premenstrual syndrome. I have used the amino acid

5-hydroxytryptophan (5HTP) instead of traditional antidepressants to help with mild to moderate depression. I have also used the amino acid L-theanine for those suffering from anxiety with positive results.

Exercise Caution

After many years of experience with supplements, I now feel that it's better to take supplements under supervision because there is an art to using the right supplement. For instance, calcium citrate is more absorbable, whereas other forms of calcium may be easy to swallow but hardly absorb and therefore are not beneficial. Magnesium glycinate, for example, is a form of magnesium that absorbs well and is less likely to cause diarrhea. Without supervision, I'm afraid that people might spend money on supplements they don't need or use the wrong ones, or use ineffective supplements at the wrong dosages and occasionally cause themselves harm. For a further discussion, see chapter 8 on food for health and wellness.

Herbal Therapy

Plant life has provided us with food and medicine. Herbs, as supplements, are used and generally perceived as something physical and used for both body and mind. The pharmaceutical industry attempts to extract the "active substance" from the plant, patent it, concentrate it, and then give it back to us as "medicine." Although beneficial, some feel that these processed medicines lose something when removed from their source, based on the principle that the whole is greater than the sum of the parts and that some important function is lost when removing a part of it. There are medical practices devoted exclusively to herbal medicine.

Some herbs are familiar to the general public. An example is echinacea, used for its immune-boosting and antibacterial effect. In our clinic and in our home, it has a great reputation for helping our sore throats and viral respiratory infections when taken right at the beginning of an episode. Turmeric, the golden-colored spice used in curry formulas, is both a food and a medicine. Did you know that turmeric contains the phytonutrient curcumin that is loaded with healing properties? It is strongly anti-inflammatory, and we use it to reduce inflammation in a variety of situations. Here are some examples. In the acute stage of an injury to a muscle, tendon, or ligament, I recommend it in combination with another herb, boswellia, to help reduce the body's inflammatory response, which can be excessive and make healing more difficult.

I prefer these herbs to the use of NSAIDs (nonsteroidal anti-inflammatory drugs) because of the negative side effects with NSAIDs. Turmeric is also used in treatment for more chronic conditions such as inflammatory arthritis or inflammatory bowel diseases such as Crohn's disease and ulcerative colitis. In addition to its anti-inflammatory effect, turmeric may be helpful with cancer because it is said to inhibit the three stages of cancer: (1) initiation, where normal cells change into precancerous cells, (2) promotion, where the initiated cancer cells begin to divide and grow, and (3) proliferation, where the growing cells rapidly divide into an observable tumor. Who would have thought that musculoskeletal injury, arthritis, inflammatory bowel disease, and cancer could have been helped from that yellow spice sitting on your shelf! For more on this subject, I will discuss a few selected herbals and how we use them in our practice for medicinal purposes in chapter 10.

Cleansing Techniques

The body needs to cleanse and purify itself from the daily grind of internal cellular metabolism as well as the outward environmental struggle with "xenobiotics": the pesticides, herbicides, hormones, synthetic medicines, heavy metals, dyes, additives, and industrial pollution in the air we breathe and the food we eat. How do we do this?

I generally think of cleansing the following ways:

1. Intestinal health—involving a daily bowel movement to remove solid waste
2. Kidney health—involving several full urinations a day to remove liquid waste
3. Lung health—involving an opportunity to breathe deeply, inhaling oxygen and exhaling carbon dioxide and toxins
4. Skin health—involving perspiration and the expression of unwanted material
5. Liver health—the liver acts on chemicals and toxic material and detoxifies them and prepares them for removal
6. Menses and the lymphatic system are additional modes of cleansing

Good health requires that these organs and organ systems stay fully functional. If blocked, all have their appropriate expression of symptoms and corresponding treatment methods to help restore their balance. For example, a delayed gastrointestinal emptying is diagnosed as constipation, and the treatment may include drinking more water, adding more fiber to the diet, and adding the Ayurvedic herbal Triphala, a preparation that is said to "tonify" the bowel.

A swollen tongue with a light purplish hue may indicate that the liver is struggling to work efficiently. This may require remedies as diverse as the herb milk thistle (silymarin) or specific vitamins, minerals, and amino acids to support its detoxification phases.

Swollen, nonpitting edema (indicated when pressing a finger into the swollen tissue does not leave an indentation in the skin) in the legs may indicate lymphedema or lymphatic obstruction. This is a condition where the fluid accumulates in the area because the lymphatic channels are blocked or working poorly and, in this case, require gentle upward stroking of the skin over the areas of swelling. This action, called "lymphatic drainage therapy," will help drain the lymph channels into the inguinal lymphatics located in the inner thigh area and help bring the swelling down.

In general, if you eat food with enough fiber, maintain adequate hydration, and exercise in a moderate and consistent fashion, you will have a natural cleansing program. However, you can see from the examples above that an individually tailored cleansing program to fit your personal needs requires an accurate diagnosis and treatment plan from a trained health practitioner.

Chiropractic Treatment

Daniel David Palmer founded chiropractic in the 1880s, and his son, B. J. Palmer, continued its development into the 1900s. It has been described as a "hands-on" manual therapy that affects the spine and musculoskeletal system. Traditionally it has been taught that the spinal vertebrae, ligaments, and tendons are intricately connected to the nerves throughout the body, which affect the blood supply, tissues, organs, and muscles of the body. If a particular bone in the spine is out of alignment for any reason (injury, strain, poor posture, poor nutrition, etc.), this is termed "subluxation," and this misalignment can be put right with a spinal-manipulation technique termed "an adjustment."

A successful adjustment is designed to restore proper functioning of the bones, which restores proper nerve function, thereby improving circulation and soft-tissue repair and allowing healing to take place in the affected area. In addition to the adjustment, many doctors of chiropractic will teach their patients proper stretching and strengthening exercises in an effort to reeducate their bodies to prevent injury or misuse. They may also include the use of nutrition and supplementation to strengthen the health of the tissues and the immune response of their patients.

Massage Therapy

This healing modality has been around since biblical times. The goal of massage is soft-tissue manipulation (muscles, tendons, ligaments, and fascia) anywhere in the body. There are over eighty styles of massage. The practitioner may use his or her hands, fingers, knuckles, elbows, feet, and instruments in an effort to create the desired therapeutic result. When we think of the relatively superficial systematic and therapeutic stroking and kneading of the body, we are referring to Swedish massage. When the practitioner presses deeply to remedy tension or pain in deeper tissues, this is appropriately called "deep-tissue massage." Different techniques are used by the practitioner, depending on his or her training and the patient's needs. Massage therapy may improve circulation (lymphatic and blood), reduce tension and spasms, bring pain relief, improve mobility, and help to lessen anxiety and depression.

Feldenkrais Method®

Dr. Moshe Feldenkrais, an engineer and physicist, developed a method of sensorimotor bodywork in an effort to rehabilitate himself after a personal injury. The method was so successful that his training and workshops became known worldwide. I had the good fortune of working with him in a workshop in Chicago, and I can attest to his gentleness, kindness, and creativity.

How does it work? The practitioner may guide his patients through a series of gentle movements either by talking them through the movements or by gently moving the hand or leg or neck. Great attention is placed on the awareness of the quality of the movement and how it affects the rest of the body. Practitioners claim that the freedom and ease of movement and the lessening of pain that come after a session is due to a reeducation of how the muscles and nerves work together to create the whole body working more synergistically. Feldenkrais can help little children with walking and sleep issues as well as the elderly with the pain of arthritis or the effects of stroke and other neurological issues, and it helps everyone to move his or her body more efficiently, comfortably, and with ease. I have a friend who swears by his weekly session to keep him in running shape, and he calls it his antiaging medicine.

Exercise

See chapter 11.

Hatha-Yoga

Yoga originated in India some three to five thousand years ago. The word "yoga" is commonly translated from Sanskrit as "union," referring to the possibility of uniting body, breath, mind, and spirit or uniting the individual soul with the universal consciousness through its wide variety of practices.

There are six major types of yoga, each with a different purpose. Perhaps the most well known is hatha-yoga, a system of exercises consisting of slow stretching movements assisted by attention to one's breathing. These movements are designed to create suppleness and strength and reduce tension and stress in all parts of the body as well as help create a sense of balanced energy, mental alertness, and the increased ability to focus and concentrate—what yogis call a "one-pointed mind." It is recommended for helping many medical conditions such as attention deficit disorder, high blood pressure, asthma, headache, backache, premenstrual syndrome, and other chronic diseases, as well as promoting the relaxation response, reducing stress, and improving self-esteem. Although we recommend hatha-yoga as a physical technique applied to the body, it may be used to affect the energy, mind, and spiritual life of the student, if he or she so desires.

Energy Level—Linking the Body to the Mind

Traditionally, there are therapies associated with the energy sheath, which is also called the "pranic sheath," and these are called "energy-medicine" techniques (see chapter 12). What these techniques have in common is that they are intended to directly affect the "energy" part of our functioning, the pranic sheath, as previously described. What follows is a brief explanation of a few of these therapies as we explore our energy tools in our toolbox of techniques.

Breathing Exercises (Pranayama)

Pranayama may be translated as "control of the life force." This life-force energy has been called "*prana*," "*chi*," "*ki*," or "vital force," depending upon which tradition you are using (see chapter 5). One way to control this energy is through the conscious regulation of our breathing patterns. We are taught that the *prana* or life force circulating throughout the energy pathways in the body is affected by breathing techniques similar to how one controls or affects the flight of a kite using the string that is attached to it. In this analogy, the kite represents the pranic (energy) vehicle circulating throughout the body, and the string represents our attempts to exercise control over this energy by working with our breathing pattern—somewhat indirect but still effective. Here are a few examples of different breathing techniques:

1. Abdominal breathing helps quiet down our "flight or fight" response to stress.
2. Diaphragmatic breathing increases the amount of air we can inhale into and exhale from our lungs and is especially helpful in respiratory disorders and when exercising.
3. *Kapalbhati* is considered a cleansing technique in which we actively exhale and passively inhale.
4. Alternate-nostril breathing is a technique that creates a sense of balance and peace and is often used for stress reduction and in preparation for meditation. (See chapter 12 on yoga and breathing for more detail.)

Relaxation Techniques

There are many methods for achieving the subjective experience of muscular relaxation and mental calmness. Most commonly, we teach our patients and students to relax their bodies by systematically moving their awareness from the tops of their heads downward through the head, neck, arms, hands, fingers, trunk, pelvis, legs, feet, and toes.

Initially, the students listen to our voice as we guide them in a systematic way to experience their bodies as above, let go of tension in that part of the body they are focusing on, and use their breathing as the vehicle that accompanies their minds as they shift from one part of the body to another. A successful session will result in lowering tension and stress, quieting the flight or fight response, and obtaining a sense of well-being and peace. It may be very effective for those with anxiety, high blood pressure, and insomnia. I think of it as an energy technique because I consider the person's awareness of his or her breathing as the key ingredient to success and link the use of breath to energy work as explained above. It is taught that relaxation is a necessary step in preparation before attempting to meditate.

Homeopathy

See chapter 13.

Acupuncture/Acupressure

Acupuncture is another powerful energy medicine. Traditional acupuncture is based on ancient Chinese theories of the flow of energy called "*chi*" as it courses through the energy pathways called "meridians." Meridians cover the body somewhat like the nerves and the blood vessels do but are said to have a functional-energetic anatomy rather than a physical presence. The theory states that these meridians provide the *chi* (life force) to the various tissues and organs of the body, allowing them to function properly. If the energy flow in a particular meridian is either blocked (stagnant) or in excess, this is considered an energy imbalance and may create disharmony or disease in the organs affected by that meridian.

How does the practitioner know which one to treat? The acupuncturist will make a diagnosis and treatment plan based upon a history of the symptoms of the patient, including a pulse and tongue examination. Based upon these findings, the practitioner decides which meridians have unbalanced energy. He or she then uses fine, filament-like needles to insert at specific points called "acupuncture points" located in the appropriate meridian to correct the energy flow. Alternatively, the practitioner may use his or her fingertips to apply sustained pressure at these points. This is called "acupressure." If the energy is blocked or stagnant, the treatment will allow the energy to flow properly again. If the energy is excessive, the treatment will reduce the energy to a proper amount. In this way, acupuncture or acupressure regulates the flow of energy to the body by restoring balance.

I have seen acupuncture help in acute situations, including the pain associated with injuries, sprains, strains, headaches, colds, and sinus infections, as well as chronic conditions such as chronic fatigue, chronic migraine headaches, arthritis, insomnia, or the effects of stress. It is also helpful for the nausea and vomiting that are side effects induced by chemotherapy.

Flower-Essence Therapy

See chapter 14.

Mental Level—the Conscious and Unconscious Mind

There are many tools to help the practitioner or patient look at the conscious and unconscious parts of the mind. In addition to the discussion below, see chapters 15 through 19 and appendix 1.

Yoga Chakra Therapy

I have listed this concept here under the mental sphere in the whole health diagram because I feel it is very useful as a psychological perspective in treatment. A more complete discussion follows under basic concepts in chapter 5. Briefly, there are different and specific psychological issues associated with each chakra. For example, chronic tonsillitis or a thyroid problem at the throat chakra may be associated with conflict about expressing yourself and saying what's really on your mind or expressing your life purpose through your job or living situation, for instance.

How do we know this? Yoga philosophy states that mental and emotional issues are actually located throughout the body. Each of the seven chakras has its own constellation of physical structure, glands, nervous tissue, and emotional life associated with it. Thus it is taught "the body reflects the mind," and a trained practitioner can help the motivated patient focus in on the underlying cause of the problem. (For a fuller discussion, see yoga-chakra medicine in chapter 5.)

Psychotherapy/Counseling

Patients may engage in the many forms of talk therapy now available. I find it helpful for patients to obtain professional help when the issues cannot be worked through by oneself or by the couple themselves. Recurring personal problems in specific situations, difficult or unhappy marriages, traumas or losses from the past, or difficult current events may trigger physical symptoms in the individual and act as impediments to one's peace of mind and spiritual development. It then becomes necessary to remove these "ball and chains" issues so that one's psychological and spiritual development can continue. Over the years, I have attempted to integrate many approaches into my work, including psychodynamic psychotherapy, gestalt therapy, family systems therapy, yoga psychology, and Chassidic philosophy. This topic will be discussed more fully with a case example in chapter 15.

Journaling

Some people prefer the healing privacy of writing in their own journal. I have seen many patients make remarkable breakthroughs on their issues of blocked grief, unexpressed anger, or indecision about their life purpose, to name a few examples. I recommend they begin with something simple and doable, such as five to fifteen minutes a day. It helps to define the topic as much as possible. I ask them to bring in their journal on the next visit and share with me by reading it to me. These people are comfortable with this request, even though they are not comfortable with the idea of one-on-one counseling. It has been a privilege for me to hear the unfolding of patients through their journals. In appendix 1, I discuss how I use my personal journal in the mornings.

Spiritual Level

The disciplines of personal prayer, contemplation, and meditation are very individualized methods for self-development and, in general, seem little understood and not used by most people.

Personal Prayer

The sages have formulated prayers with great meaning. The study of these words and the concepts they involve can be very powerful. One may also pray in such a way as to allow the words to flow from the heart spontaneously. This is called "personal prayer." I find prayer to be a very powerful healing modality, and as with all the healing modalities, I only suggest it if the patient is open to it.

For certain patients, especially in very difficult situations, I help them "jump-start" into a personal prayer that fits their temperament. It can begin simply with just a few words of sharing about the physical or emotional difficulty or hardship they are experiencing and end with a heartfelt request for help or healing. It helps to have a regular prayer time so that your habit becomes a support for you. It also helps to find a space where you feel safe and that has few distractions so you can focus your mind on what you want to say and open your heart to your innermost feelings. See appendix 1 for more on personal prayer.

Contemplation and Study

The ancient traditions that I am aware of have philosophies, scriptures, folktales, folklore, and wisdom handed down through the generations in both written and oral form. I believe that the disciplined study of these materials can help you develop the psychological/spiritual part of yourself. For example, in appendix 1 under the heading "Spiritual Contemplative Work," I use the example of working with a concept called "acts of kindness," and I discuss a "gratitude" practice. There are many topics to think about and work with, according to the needs of your personality. Pick one and begin applying it to yourself for a few minutes a day. Over time and with patience, you can actually change a part of yourself for the better. (Fake it until you make it.) This is very fulfilling.

Meditation

I address this tool in more detail in chapter 19. Briefly, where contemplation involves thinking and working through a subject, the form of meditation I am discussing involves pure concentration and not thinking. It requires sitting in a secure position, regulating the breath, and then being able to concentrate on a sound (*mantra*). Through training, you can condition yourself to follow the sound and establish yourself in your "witness" and let go of the thinking part of the mind. The results can lead to physical healing as in lowering blood pressure or reducing tension headaches. Meditation can also bring peace of mind as in less anxiety and worry.

Another benefit of meditation is the acquisition of clarity of consciousness as in the quiet, subtle, and powerful experience of *bituel*—a Hebrew word for self-less, i.e., the experience of letting go of our everyday conscious preoccupation with the "thingness" of the world as we come a bit closer to the divine within us. In this state, we have the privilege to "know" things about ourselves and receive or intuit information from the external world. We acquire the possibility of becoming a vessel for divine guidance to flow through us, inform us, and help us make the right choices for a full, exact, and fulfilling life.

Conclusion

The techniques in the whole health diagram bring cohesiveness to our thinking when we evaluate and treat a patient. We can choose to intervene from the physical, energetic, psychological, or spiritual domain, as the person needs and desires.

5

Yoga-Chakra Theory of Medicine

Of all the perspectives I am privileged to use in the practice of holistic medicine, yoga-chakra theory is one of my favorites.

Figure 5-1. Chakra illustration.

What is a chakra? In yoga texts, energy is said to travel throughout the body in energy pathways or channels called "*nadis*." A chakra is actually that location in the body where major energy pathways (*nadis*) intersect. There are seven chakras in the body, and each is associated with its own particular constellation of glands, nervous tissue, energy, and emotional issues. (See figure 5-1.) This is a very different concept from Western medicine where the body is physical tissue, and we are not concerned with consciousness attached to it.

In yoga, it is taught that "the body reflects the mind" because our mental and emotional issues are actually located throughout our body as exemplified by the chakra theory. If this is true, a trained practitioner can help the motivated patient focus on the underlying cause of the problem by being familiar with this theory. Let's explore this together.

First Chakra (Theme Is Survival)

This is defined as the root chakra. It is the area of influence that involves the rectum, perineum, and base of the spine. The energy, if unbalanced, affects the large intestine, rectum, coccyx, and hamstrings. The mental issues associated with that area deal with life and death, good and bad, fear and security.

Case Example: Survival or Not

Larry is a thirty-six-year-old single male having difficulty at work. He fears losing his job. He suffers from ulcerative colitis and hemorrhoids. His dreams are full of violence and catastrophe. The diagnosis is unresolved first-chakra issues, causing unbalanced energy at the root chakra, which then affects his organs at that location.

Treatment

We begin with recommending yoga postures that bring awareness to this area, such as the forward bend. Another exercise called *Mula Bandha* (a rectal contraction exercise) may help relax the tension in the area. Breathing techniques and homeopathic remedies or acupuncture will help correct the energy imbalance, and a little stress reduction or counseling all help him to shift out of the "life or death" mode of functioning that underlies the problem. The opportunity here requires the healer to view this illness as an expression of the underlying fearful question, "Will I continue to exist or not if I lose my job?" In this perspective, this issue must be addressed and transformed in order to obtain lasting relief from the symptom and allow the body to heal.

Second Chakra (Theme Is Right Use of Sensuality and Sexuality)

The focus of this chakra is located at the pelvic plexus, above the genitals, near the bladder and lower lumbar spine. The physical structures influenced by this chakra include the pelvic organs, quadriceps, and low back. The psychological expression in this area includes the integration of our sexual identity and sexual self-image, our ability to experience sensuality and pleasure, and our drive to procreate.

Case Example: Cystitis, Indecisiveness, and Anger

Shelia is forty-two with a history of chronic candidiasis and cystitis. Antibiotics would help for a while, but the symptoms would return. Dietary advice and remedies also helped temporarily. Why wouldn't the positive effects of these treatments hold up? She began to confront a frustrated desire in a significant relationship. She also acknowledged that she was angry. We explored some of her thoughts and feelings about this person in her life. She talked about issues including her femininity, her desire, her self-image, and a course of right action within a longstanding but uncommitted relationship.

As we spoke, I realized that her indecisiveness, frustration, and anger were being somatized into her body! In her case, she agreed with this interpretation when I brought it up to her. As her treatment unfolded and she worked these things out, the remedies and treatments began to take hold. She stayed symptom-free for longer periods. In the end, she felt comfortable with her decision about the relationship and with herself. Her energy was improved in this area, and her body could heal.

Third Chakra (Theme Is Right Use of Personal Power)

The focus of this chakra is located at the solar plexus. The solar-plexus chakra is located above the navel and behind the stomach. "Solar" relates to a fiery kind of energy, as it is taught that the "home" of the fiery principle in the body is in the solar-plexus area of the body. (We will discuss the energies of earth, water, fire, air, and space in chapter 6 on Ayurvedic medicine.)

Physically, the fire energy at this chakra is used to transform the world around us by converting food into energy and body structure. The organs associated with these functions are the stomach, liver, spleen, small intestine, adrenals, and pancreas. Besides digestion, the fruits of this chakra are intelligence, alertness, and mental sharpness. Issues that press for resolutions are passive versus aggressive, domination versus submission, top dog versus underdog, and competition promoting "I" versus cooperation promoting "we." The energy here influences our whole body and is ideally meant for the right use of one's power being refocused downward toward survival (first chakra) and right gratification of the senses (second chakra), or upward toward the heart's expression of love (fourth chakra) and one's higher self-expression (fifth chakra).

Case Example: Abdominal Pain and Competition

A man of fifty-five with a red complexion and balding on top of his head complained of digestive problems, including gas, abdominal pain, bloating, and diarrhea alternating with constipation. During the history taking, he revealed he was very stressed while working long hours on a big project. He admitted to being very tense and impatient, often losing his temper with the people around him, and indeed, he appeared very intense during the interview. In my mind I was thinking, "Third-chakra issues affecting third-chakra organs." In his case, I was looking for any pathology in his gallbladder, liver, or upper and lower gastrointestinal tract. Together, we created a treatment plan beginning with blood work, stool samples, and possibly some ultrasound studies. I always like to have a conventional diagnosis to work with because I feel that both the patient and the healer need to be grounded in knowing what they are dealing with. This promotes trust and helps the treatment plan.

Now how to cool him down and have him refocus his fire appropriately? Simply taking an anti-inflammatory or an antibiotic might remove a symptom for now, but I would expect his overproduction of fire at the third chakra would simply create more pathology with the possibility of worsening symptoms as time progressed. The task was to reeducate both his body and his mind.

We began his reeducation by teaching him a breathing technique called "diaphragmatic breathing" (see chapter 12). This enabled him to decrease the intensity of his response to challenging situations in his life. How does this work? Diaphragmatic breathing helps us to decrease the stress response we call "flight or fight." I discuss this in more detail in chapter 15.

We next used one of the psychospiritual tools in the physician's toolbox. I introduced the idea that he could approach his work in a friendlier way by valuing assertion, competence, and cooperation rather than aggression, domination, and winning—in other words, assertion but not aggression, and cooperation and teamwork rather than winning or losing. His face lit up, the light bulb went on, and you could palpate the excitement of discovery as he glimpsed the real possibility of transforming something about himself that really needed to change.

Fourth Chakra (Theme Is Loving Others)

Located between the breasts and underneath the sternum, the fourth (heart) chakra is associated with the organs in the chest, including the breasts, lungs, and heart. The theme of giving love and nurturance and reaching out to embrace and love others makes this area the focus of compassionate relatedness.

Case Example: Respiratory Infection and Heart Disease

Mary was worried. She had been tired for some time. The chronic respiratory infection just wouldn't go away. She was tired of doing so much for others but felt too guilty to say no to their requests. At the end of the day, her chest actually ached. We began treatment with a dietary and supplement program to help strengthen her immune system.

The flip side to selfless service is self-sufficiency. Mary needed to create a boundary—a self that could be protected by her immune system against a virus, a bacteria, or a person's request, if need be. Toward this end, she was given the flower essence Centaury (see chapter 14) to help her say no when appropriate. Briefly, Centaury helps strengthen one's emotional boundary resulting in a greater sense of self with the ability to be more independent.

Her father had the opposite problem. A history of heart disease in an intensely achieving man suggests a story of stagnant development—the inability of third-chakra energy to ascend and express itself through love and kindness going outward to others. And so the heart, deprived of its energy and rightful actions, begins a slow process of tightening and closure (arteriosclerosis). In his case, the yoga postures such as cobra, fish, and other chest openers can expand the chest wall and promote the emotional experience of openheartedness.

Fifth Chakra (Theme Is Receptivity and Self-Expression)

The focus of this energy, the throat chakra, is found in the hollow of the throat opposite the seventh cervical vertebra. The organs affected include the thyroid, larynx, tonsils, salivary glands, and soft tissue of the neck. There are several themes at play at this chakra. They include receptivity, surrender, the ability to take in nurturance and love, and the capacity for devotion, faith, creativity, and self-expression. That is a lot to swallow! Imagine bending your head backward. The feeling at the throat is one of exposure and vulnerability. With practice, this can transform into the pleasant sensation of surrender and trust.

In my practice, I have seen that clearing up unresolved communication in relationships often helps thyroid problems, especially in women.

Case Example: The Resolution of a Thyroid Nodule

A married woman in her thirties with three young children came to the office complaining about the discovery of a thyroid nodule in her neck. She didn't want the diagnostic biopsy or thyroid extract that was being recommended. I brought up the topic of the throat chakra and asked her if she had difficulty in expressing verbally what was on her mind. She responded by telling me the frustration she was having with her husband in her marriage. We proceeded with some counseling sessions. Over time, I witnessed that nodule completely disappear after she was able to express verbally to her husband what she had been holding back and not saying for years.

In this case, we speculate that the blocked throat-chakra function of verbal self-expression had affected the energy in this region. This dysfunctional energy had affected the thyroid tissue, which manifested in the symptom of a thyroid nodule. In other people, I have seen this blocked or unbalanced energy manifest as chronic tonsillitis or external neck problems. I've seen neck tension and stiff-necked people improve when the person begins to "turn" away (from stubbornness) and see the other person's point of view!

Figure 5-2. Shoulder-stand posture.

Do-It-Yourself Psychotherapy

Here is a personal example of an issue that was tucked away in my own throat chakra. In the past, while practicing yoga, I put myself into the shoulder-stand posture and steadied my breath. (See figure 5-2.) In this posture, you are upside down, and the head is flexed up against the chest. (Try this feeling by sitting or standing and gently allowing your head to rotate forward and downward so that your chin is resting on your chest.)

As I relaxed and watched for any feelings or thoughts that might come up, I began to feel the sensation of choking. I was shocked to remember and reexperience the feeling in my neck associated with an emotional era of my life in high school.

I remembered specific people, faces, and situations—all associated with the feeling of being physically and emotionally intimidated.

Now comes the healing part of the story. As I repeated the posture slowly, over a period of time, the memories and feelings came and went. Each time I repeated this posture along with breathing and observation, the sensation of choking became less and less. All the unpleasant memories lost their emotional strength, and indeed, the sensation in my neck became that of simply being stretched on the back side and compressed on the front side.

This experience with my neck reminded me of a deeper function of hatha-yoga beyond the benefits of stretching—the possibility of self-therapy! If you so choose, you can put yourself in a posture, relax, breathe, and be open to whatever "unfinished business" comes up into your awareness that was secretly embedded in that part of your body at that chakra! Now realize this. Since your yoga practice can be designed to practice postures that represent all the chakras, you have the opportunity to use your body/mind for personal growth anywhere, anytime throughout your life. Free therapy!

Sixth Chakra (Theme Is Intuition/Spiritual Receptivity)

The last chakra we will discuss, often referred to as the "third eye," is located at the forehead between the eyebrows, in association with the pineal and pituitary glands. Chronic sinusitis, migraine headaches, seizures, and difficulties with vision may represent some of the physical problems that arise from imbalance at this chakra. Wisdom, intuition, and discrimination are skills cultivated at this chakra and are considered high-functioning mental skills in combination with spiritual receptivity. With proper third-eye functioning, a person is able to discern his or her personal truth, choose fulfilling personal and professional relationships, and, in general, make life-path choices that bring lasting satisfaction and peace of mind.

We promote the healthy functioning of this area with techniques such as hatha-yoga postures (tree, headstand), a premeditative breathing technique (chapter 12), prayer (appendix 1), contemplation, and meditation (chapter 19). Sometimes, a psychological problem can block the channels of spiritual receptivity and may have to be cleared up before the above techniques can be effective (see chapter 15). In that case, a person may use some counseling or journaling alongside his or her meditation practice.

Insight/Seeing Within

I remember a young lady in her thirties sitting in front of me, complaining about her recurrent sinusitis and her near-everyday headache. As I sat and listened to her, I asked her to take a few gentle breaths as I formulated a question for her. I began explaining to her that the brow chakra is the home of the so-called third eye, which means that there is an intuitive seeing or understanding function that takes place there. Perhaps her headache symptoms were indicating that her insight might be blocked, and I wondered if she could gently relax with this idea and look (inside) to see if anything came up into her awareness about being blocked or stuck.

I had barely finished this suggestion when she began crying softly and stated, "I know what it is. It's my job. I hate my job. I've known this for a long time, and I just haven't faced the truth about it." The insight was sudden and complete. We proceeded to explore it for a while, and by the end of the session, her face softened, she appeared more relaxed, and she sounded cautiously hopeful. She had the appearance of someone who felt relieved with her discovery, and hopefully, this will have an empowering effect on her physical symptoms, i.e., the headache will no longer be "needed" to draw her attention to any sixth-chakra unresolved issues.

Summary

This has been a brief description of a very complex subject. In my opinion, the yoga-chakra theory of medicine provides the healer a magnificent perspective to understand and readily see how a physical symptom and the psychology associated with it are expressed together in a specific area of the body through an energetic pathway. Therefore, at any level of the body, we view a complete picture of how the body/mind functions, which allows us to diagnose and treat an illness or help improve wellness.

6

Ayurveda, the Science of Life and Longevity

Introduction

In ancient India, a philosophy known as *Sankhya* (see chapter 3) attempted to explain the nature of how physical reality came to be. Two famous offspring developed from this philosophy—the sister sciences of yoga and Ayurveda. Ayurveda is the medical application, and yoga was intended to be the self-care, practical, body/mind-oriented science.

Both practices were developed to help humanity in response to the progression of illness, as illness was seen to be an impediment to the evolution of consciousness. Both encourage the ability of people to observe themselves and therefore empower one to restore or balance his or her physical, emotional, and spiritual health. Apparently, ancient practitioners lived long and vital lives by using self-observation and self-balance. Let's see if we can learn a few basic principles of Ayurveda to help with our self-care and the health of others. Please note that Ayurveda is a very complex philosophy, science, and practice, and from my limited perspective, I'd like to offer you a small taste to whet your appetite.

History

Historically, the science of Ayurveda originated in India and then moved to China as the five-element theory involving earth, water, fire, wind, and space. It then traveled to Persia, Greece, and back to India where it continued to be refined. The science is taught in Ayurvedic medical schools in India today.

Scope

I was taught that the seven major divisions of Ayurveda are internal medicine; surgery; ear, nose, and throat; pediatrics; toxicology; rejuvenation; and spiritual healing through the use of mantras and other techniques.

Basic Philosophy

The *Sankhya* philosophy offers an explanation of how physical reality comes into existence. As part of a complex explanation, it describes the evolution of five elements that describe the world around and inside us: earth (the solid principle), water (fluid, liquid principle), fire (the hot transformative principle), air (that which moves things), and space (no-thingness, ether-like). Ayurveda further refined and simplified these elements into the famous three-stranded principle known as *tridhatu*, meaning "three supporting structures" (known popularly as *tridosha*), as follows:

- Kapha (combining the elements of water and earth)
- Pitta (the element of fire)
- Vata (combining the elements of air [motion] and space)

According to Ayurveda, our physical and mental selves are organized into constitutions reflecting a predominance of two of the three *dhatus* (supporting structures). Let's have a look and see if you recognize yourself in any of the constitutions we will now describe.

Kapha Constitution and Appearance

The properties of the elements making up Kapha are cold, wet, and stable. In nature we think of mountains, big trees, and big bodies of water as earthy and stable. In the body we think of our bones, muscles, and mucous membranes as representing the stable, solid structural part of us.

Kapha people may appear large, muscular to heavy, big-boned, or plump with a tendency to overweight. The skin is soft and smooth with large brown eyes, thick hair, and large white teeth. They are slow in action, fertile, jolly, graceful, loving, stable, and calm. They bring a sense of cohesiveness and security to those around them, as their personality reflects stability and solidness. A Kapha person will do his or her duties with regularity while eating and sleeping at the same time and same place.

The Kapha season is winter (cold), and the Kapha time of our twenty-four-hour day is 6:00 a.m. to 10:00 a.m. and 6:00 p.m. to

10:00 p.m. Childhood is the Kapha age where bone and mass are added quickly in the formation of structure (age one to sixteen).

Imbalance

Kapha is unbalanced by overeating or eating foods that stimulate mucus production (sweets, bananas, dairy, wheat, meat), oversleeping, cold weather, or inactivity. When this happens, Kapha will become an exaggeration of its normal tendencies. Slow becomes inactive. Stability turns to stagnation, lethargy, dullness, and depression. Steadfastness becomes stubbornness and procrastination. In the body, imbalance will exaggerate the earthy elements expressing itself as tumors, fibroids, growths, and weight gain. The mucous membranes, representing the watery elements, will become affected and promote asthma, bronchitis, sinusitis, tonsillitis, ear infections, upper-respiratory infections, and arthritis. They are all considered Kapha diseases.

Balancing Kapha

As stated above, ear infections, tonsillitis, bronchitis, asthma, and arthritis (all involving wetness and moisture) may be the consequences of too much Kapha. These conditions may be reduced or eliminated by reducing the foods that promote mucus in the body such as wheat, dairy, and sweets to excess. It is taught that foods which are less than fresh, such as frozen or canned or older stale foods stimulate the body to create mucus—probably as a cleansing response.

After applying these dietary interventions, I have seen the tendency to childhood ear infections completely clear up after years of antibiotic usage no longer helped. Every category of food has its Kapha influences. In the fruit category, bananas aggravate Kapha (think of the mushy consistency of a banana, which is similar to earth and water; the same with peanut butter, for that matter); on the other hand, apples, especially green ones, decrease mucus. For grains, cooked oats make mucus, whereas dry oats (granola) or millet are acceptable: the same with vegetables, meats, beans, etc. With a little Ayurvedic study, we can work with these conditions and help reduce or eliminate symptoms. (This topic is covered in more detail in chapter 6.)

Overcoming Inertia, Depression, and Head Congestion

A muscular mountain of a man who is a bodyworker in our clinic is usually a jolly, softer, and loving colleague. On occasion, he will come to work looking glassy-eyed, slowed down, heavy, lethargic, slightly depressed, and complaining of head congestion. If allowed to continue, he will miss one week of work with an upper-respiratory infection. Invariably, the cause for him is eating too much (Kapha tendency) after dinner (Kapha time), too many sweets (Kapha food), followed by inactivity—all worsened in winter. If he cuts down the food, adds some spices (Pitta fire), moderates the sweets, and walks in the evening, the congestion clears up, the lethargy disappears, and he makes the transformation from human mountain to human being right in front of our eyes!

Pitta Constitution and Appearance

The properties of the element of Pitta are hot, oily, and irritable, representing the energy of fire (the color red). When we think of fire, we think of burning flames, heat, and light. Pitta is the energy that transforms one thing into another. In the body, the food that we have eaten is changed into energy with the help of digestive enzymes. Fire energy is said to express itself via these enzymes. Pitta also affects the health of the skin, eyes, and circulatory system. In the mind, Pitta energy helps an idea that is formulated become expressed. This fire represents the "lighting up" of insight—popularly represented as a light bulb coming on that gives clarity and understanding to a situation. Pitta may have a reddish complexion with coppery skin and nails. The men may bald on top with both sexes appearing angular, hyperactive, and perceptive, and exhibiting an acute intelligence going straight to the point. No beating around the bush with Pitta. They are active and intense, busily getting things done. They are competitive and assertive. You will know what the Pitta person stands for, as shyness is not his or her trait.

The Pitta time is 10:00 a.m. to 2:00 p.m. (high noon with warmth and light) and 10:00 p.m. to 2:00 a.m. The fire season is summer, and the age when Pitta is dominant is sixteen to forty (engaged in transforming the world through action).

Imbalance

Pitta is unbalanced by influences that exaggerate its natural tendencies, such as external heat; stimulants such as coffee, spices, garlic, pepper, ginger, alcohol, chocolate, and cigarettes; overexertion; overworking; anger; and stressful competition. When this happens, Pitta will become an exaggeration of its normal tendencies. Physically, we may see that the fire behind transformation now becomes destructive and begins to "burn" the individual, producing inflammation. The skin becomes red, hot, itchy, burning, and inflamed. Inflammatory conditions such as acid reflux, gastritis, colitis, gallbladder problems, and high blood pressure may result. In the mind, focus and intensity turn to irritability, impatience, and anger. They become quite capable of "burning" themselves or others with their words or behaviors. Competition and assertion turn to aggression, and "getting things done" becomes workaholism. This may be accompanied by a decrease in memory and mental functioning. How often have you seen a focused, intelligent, well-meaning, and healthy person become too intense, irritable, and impatient, looking red-faced, flushed with anger, and suffering from some type of inflammatory disorder? This is called "Pitta aggravation."

Mary Heats Up!

Mary is an intelligent sixty-four-year-old professional. She presented with the symptoms of burning and swelling in her face. She had tried many medications, and they would initially help, but the relief was only temporary, and the symptoms would return in full force. Her history suggests a Pitta aggravation.

On observation, Mary's face was indeed swollen and red, especially around her eyes, forehead, and cheeks. She spoke of her symptoms being aggravated by sunlight, coffee, and spices (foods that create heat). She was very stressed in her life about a personal issue and spoke angrily about it. As I listened to her, I noticed that she was wearing a red dress (the color of Pitta) and carrying her things in a red bag.

She corrected me and said very matter-of-factly, "No, Dr. Gore, the color is hot pink!"

I thought to myself, "Burning red rash, impatience, irritability, anger, worse from heat, and dressed in hot pink! This is a case of Pitta imbalance—too much fire."

Balancing Pitta

I made the following suggestions:

1. Avoid foods that increase heat, like alcohol and chocolate and spices such as pepper, cumin, and ginger, whereas foods such as raw leafy greens, apples, pears, milk, cream, and rice can cool things down. (See chapter 9.)
2. Avoid stimulants like coffee and cigarettes.
3. Avoid direct sunlight, overheating, and strenuous exercise (increases heat) and seek out cool air or water, outdoor nature, and natural beauty to calm the fire energy down.
4. Take the homeopathic remedy Apis, made from the honeybee. (See chapter 13 on homeopathy.) This remedy is indicated for hot, inflamed, and red conditions.
5. Lastly we discussed the idea that in general, the body and the mind communicate with each other, and in her case, her anger was being internalized into her body and exacerbating her tendency toward inflammation. If that was true, she needed to find a healthy and productive way of expressing it, transforming it, or letting it go.

Mary Balances Her Fire

Mary returned a week later, smiling and looking a bit less red (no more hot pink!). Her face was noticeably less swollen, and she felt less itchy. She was less fatigued, and she felt more optimistic about the personal situation in her life that had been so upsetting. She reported that there was one day when her symptoms became aggravated. This happened when she went out in the sun and had one cup of coffee.

Her symptoms quickly improved when she cooled off and kept out of the sunlight. For the most part, she followed the treatment plan we had set up for her. This had the following effect on her: she said that for the first time in her life, she felt some control over these issues and was excited to learn more about her Ayurvedic constitution. It was my impression that her natural curiosity was stimulated through the process of using her symptoms to learn about herself, and she was moved from within to discover that she, herself, could actually affect her health in a positive way.

Vata Constitution and Appearance

The properties of the elements making up Vata are a combination of *vayu* (cold, dry, irregular, active, and unstable) and *akasha* (empty and dark). Think of wind inside a space where movement and flowing energy rule the person's body/mind. If earth is stable and regular, wind is unstable and irregular. If fire is hot and light, *akasha* (space) is dark and empty, void-like. Physically, the person is likely to be chilly, smaller, thin, or slight of build or wiry. The skin may be rough and dry, darkened, wrinkled, and shows many veins. The hair is dry, and the eyes are small and darting around as the person may speak with a weak or broken voice. All habits are light, quick, and irregular (like the wind). On one hand, these traits encourage creativity and enthusiasm, such as energetically writing poetry or coming up with new ideas. Imbalance, on the other hand, encourages daydreaming, agitation, dissipation, hastiness, changeability, loss of focus, and anxiety. Similar to the wind, irregularity is the norm, as they have difficulty sticking to regularly scheduled times for eating, sleeping, exercising, working, etc.

Vata energy rules from 2:00 a.m. to 6:00 a.m. and from 2:00 p.m. to 6:00 p.m. Vata energies are magnified in the fall season in which wind and change predominate. Vata is more noticeable as we age and especially after forty. This is because the natural progression of aging is to dry out (dehydration), lose structure (bone and muscle, i.e., Kapha), lose our digestive fire (Pitta—literally lose the ability to produce hydrochloric acid), lose memory (Pitta), become cold (loss of Pitta), and kind of wither away (ugh). Do not be discouraged, however! Vata can be balanced and harnessed for graceful aging.

Imbalance

Vata is unbalanced by influences that exaggerate its natural tendencies. The following foods stimulate Vata: pungent (such as onions, garlic, radish, ginger, and cumin), astringent (beans, apples, pears, cabbage, and broccoli), bitter (romaine lettuce, spinach, turmeric, and lemon rind), and foods that stimulate its cold and dry qualities (such as raw vegetables and cold and dry foods, as in dried fruit), as well as stimulants such as coffee, nicotine, and alcohol.

Foods that balance Vata are sweet (milk, cream, butter, and rice), sour (lemons, cheese, yogurt, grapes, and vinegar), salt, warm soups, and good hydration as well as avoiding stimulants such as alcohol, caffeine, and nicotine. Vata is also unbalanced by the following: irregularity in eating and sleeping and suppression of natural urges such as delaying urination and defecation, staying up too late, not enough rest, noises and speaking loudly, cold and dry winds, bouncing around in cars, worrying, and instability in relationships or jobs.

When this happens, Vata will become an exaggeration of its normal self. Physically, dry skin becomes cracked, and gastrointestinal difficulties may appear. I was taught that there are five Vata energy patterns, and when the natural downward-directed Vata energy (*apana vayu*) becomes blocked, it reverses direction and rises in the body. This phenomenon becomes responsible for many gastrointestinal symptoms such as constipation, gas, and bloating after eating. This rising energy may also adversely affect the organ systems higher up in the body such as causing arrhythmias in the heart, or sinusitis in the sinuses, or headache, dizziness, and anxiety in the head. Separately, sleep becomes a problem, and insomnia is common. The whole makeup appears restless, nervous (windy), and spacey (*akasha*): first here, now there. One may say about a person, "He or she doesn't have his or her feet on the ground. The person forgets appointments and becomes easily distracted." Productive creativity loses out to daydreaming, dissipation, hastiness, and instability. Enthusiasm turns to anxiety and fear.

Balancing Vata

Miss D., a middle-aged teacher, came in as a revisit. I had known and admired her for years. She had become a student of her own health and was always ready to discover how she could learn more and improve her health with natural tools whenever possible. She was naturally tall and thin, but today she appeared thin and gaunt, and although she was middle-aged, she looked tired and withered as she softly complained of anxiety from the combined stresses of a difficult work environment and the necessity of selling her house. She also complained of chilliness and dizziness, and she was having some problems sleeping. It wasn't hard to see that these stresses had pushed her over the edge, and her Vata was out of balance.

I essentially became her coach and reminded her of what she already knew: that in these stressful times, she needed to attend to her Vata constitution and balance it. She nodded in affirmation, and we came up with the following Ayurvedic prescription.

Balance Cold and Dry with Warm and Wet

The first step is to address her cold and dryness. I did this by suggesting ways of creating warmth and moisture (juiciness). The first suggestion involves food because food is such a powerful tool for balancing. Start with hydration. Drink six to eight glasses of lukewarm water a day while avoiding cold drinks or cold food for that matter, because in her case, warm soups and hot milk drinks add the qualities of warmth and wetness. If taken at night, the milk can act as a relaxing and sleep-inducing drink. I had one patient who discovered she could calm her anxiety by drinking a mixture of milk and bananas. These foods are strongly Kapha and are a natural balance to Vata. Also, the addition of sweet, sour, and salty foods will balance Vata (see chapter 9). Next, lifestyle suggestions may help, such as making sure she dresses warmly in cool climes and avoids exposure to dry, cold, and windy weather that characterizes some winter days. One Vata-balancing therapy involves taking a warm bath or shower followed by rubbing warm sesame oil into the hands and feet before going to sleep at night.

Balance Motion and Instability with Grounding and Quietude

Imagine a chilly, windy day where everything becomes stirred up. Now imagine the wind dying down and the sun coming out; it's pleasantly warm, and it's absolutely still. That visualization is what we are trying to achieve for the body and the mind of someone in Vata imbalance. Anything that promotes grounding will pacify instability. One suggestion is to walk quietly with an even pace and concentrate on the feet, making contact with the earth. Another variation is to walk as above and focus on your breath with inhalation coming up from the ground through the feet up into the body followed by exhalation down through the body and out the feet into the ground. Another suggestion is to learn and practice yoga postures that promote the feeling of groundedness such as the standing or sitting postures. Also helpful are mindfulness exercises such as simply sitting or standing with an emphasis on being with yourself in stillness accompanied by remembering to breathe. Along these lines, specific breathing exercises for calming the mind and the body (chapter 12) and/or learning how to meditate (chapter 19) can be learned.

Other important recommendations to balance the inherent instability of Vata include internalizing the idea of regularity. Eat your meals at the same times each day. Go to sleep and awaken at the same times each twenty-four-hour period. Begin the workday at the same time, and work a consistent schedule, not a flexible schedule. Listen to classical music with its inherent repetitive structure rather than jazz, where free-form creativity reigns. As I write these suggestions for Vata, I can feel myself grounding and becoming still!

Balance Emptiness/Darkness with Love, Inner Light, and Purpose

I recommended filling the emptiness (*akasha*) with love. A loving relationship fills the void. In her case, I suggested a regular and scheduled time for physical love every day, such as a hug from a person, holding a pet, or working her garden with her hands. Notice the aspect of physical touch, because soothing physical contact is grounding to Vata. I had a patient whose words and actions reminded me of a human butterfly. Here, there, and everywhere! But when her husband hugged her or just held her hand, she transformed into a centered, grounded soul. Love through touch!

Also, in a slightly different vein, if she could find work or other meaningful activity that creates a sense of deep fulfillment and purpose, this would go a long way toward filling the void. This is true for all of us, but in Vata, it specifically calms the body/mind.

A final suggestion would be to develop the spiritual side of herself to connect to something greater that could light up her inner darkness. Many of my patients will use a personal prayer (see appendix 1) or spiritual reading or an activity that they feel "enlightens" their soul. In her case, in the evening, when physical darkness prevails, such a practice would help her feel centered and avoid the anxiety that accompanies falling into the abyss of excess Vata.

Achieve Physical Health, Peace of Mind, and Clarity of Consciousness

The basic concepts that I have shared with you have provided me with the opportunity as a physician to reach specific goals both in patient care and my own health: that of physical health, peace of mind, and clarity of consciousness. What exactly do these concepts mean? We will explore the concept of physical health in part two, peace of mind in part three, and clarity of consciousness in part four of this book.

As previously mentioned, physical health refers to our bodies. We deserve to have a body that is capable of supporting a lifestyle of movement, productivity, and mental and emotional growth and become a suitable receptacle for the soul housed within it. Let's explore this topic.

Part Two

Physical Health

In this section, I want to cover two topics that I find invaluable for creating physical health for the body: food and exercise, as well as the powerful healing subject of energy medicine. In chapter 7, I will speak about the "how" of eating. In chapter 8, I will briefly discuss different foods and why I find them valuable for health and wellness. I will then visit the topic of Ayurvedic food therapy in chapter 9. In chapter 10, I will discuss how herbs and botanicals are used as medicine. In chapter 11, I discuss my "golden rules" of exercise with the aim of focusing on simple ideas that I find to be helpful and user-friendly. I then include a transitional section of the book covering the topic of energy medicine, because energy medicine can affect the body and the mind and therefore serves as a bridge between physical health and peace of mind. In chapter 12, I speak about my experience with energy medicine, followed by an introduction to homeopathy in chapter 13 and flower-essence therapy in chapter 14.

7

Eating with Consciousness

Basic Considerations

1. Approach the Food with Mindfulness

I SUGGEST THAT THE eating experience should feel grounding and reinforce a sense of wholeness, if not holiness. How to begin training ourselves this way? Begin by asking yourself, where did this food come from? If it's corn, visualize that it came from a field. If you're about to eat an orange, which visualization feels better to you: visualizing an orchard, a wooden crate, or spacing out and eating it? Here are some other examples: butter comes from the milk of a cow, fish come from oceans or freshwater lakes, carrots come from the earth, and almonds grow in trees. Feel the connection between what you are about to eat and the reality of the world from which it came.

2. Say a Brief Prayer

Thank Spirit for the food. I believe this is easier to visualize when we are eating foods connected to nature rather than foods processed and presented in cans or packages; however, everything has its place and begs our gratitude. After all, cans are part of creation, too! Along these lines, in my experience saying a prayer or giving some semblance of gratitude before eating helps accomplish two things. First, it slows down the unconscious gulping-down-the-food habit so that we can chew the food thoroughly. Secondly, this pause allows us the opportunity to remind ourselves to use the food for energy to sustain our body/mind for our purpose in life. Traditions state that this is a way to "elevate" or spiritualize the food and add holiness to the meal.

3. Remember to Breathe

Begin to coordinate breathing gently and naturally with eating, or simply remember to breathe. Have you ever experienced that it is difficult to eat, breathe, and talk all at the same time? Eating is often communal, which serves the wonderful functions of promoting loving relationships, encouraging selfless giving, setting structure to our lives, and more. Nevertheless, I believe we must take some moments for ourselves during the meal to focus inward and become one with our eating, and that requires a mindfulness that breathing can provide.

4. Chew the Food

Train yourself to chew your food for a while and not gulp the food down. This grinding process creates smaller particles of food for your digestive organs to deal with. It also allows the food to mix with the saliva from the mouth. This is important because digestion begins in the mouth, as the food needs to mix with saliva to become alkaline before going down into the stomach where it becomes acidic.

Did you know that the process of chewing aids in liver health? The liver is an important organ for digestion. In the office, as part of the mouth exam, I look at patients' tongues. If the liver is stressed, the tongue will show teeth marks on its sides, indicating that it is swollen and is pressing against the teeth. This condition is called "scalloped tongue." My teacher quoted his teacher, who said, "The liver has no teeth," meaning that we had to chew our food to help the digestive process, including the liver.

I can't tell you how many times I have looked into patients' mouths, spotted a scalloped tongue, and asked, "Do you chew or gulp your food?"

Almost always, they look up with a surprised look on their face and say, "How did you know? I eat really quickly."

Chewing thirty-three times for thirty-three mouthfuls equals one meal, according to Ayurvedic theory. You can start with chewing one or two mouthfuls per meal this way and slowly work your way up to a chewing habit that is comfortable and that you can live with.

Please note that besides being an aid to digestion, chewing your food thoroughly is an excellent weight-loss technique because you slow down your eating, feel satisfied earlier in the meal, and end up eating less food.

5. Taste the Food

Did you know that your tongue is equipped with taste buds that will let you know a lot about the food you eat? Ayurvedic taste pharmacology is built around the idea that foods have differing effects on the body/mind, and these effects are associated with the tastes of sweet, sour, salty, pungent, astringent, and bitter. (See Ayurvedic food therapy in chapter 9.) Therefore, your taste buds can guide you in your food selection, especially when you are trying to balance your Ayurvedic constitution as discussed in chapter 6.

For example, if you feel anxious, the taste of brown rice reflects the earthy quality of "sweet" and brings with it a feeling of calm. If you feel depressed, spices such as turmeric and cumin will add the quality of "fire" and "air" and help decrease the feeling of depression. In addition, I have experienced that while focusing on taste, this mindfulness can bring another health dividend—an awareness of the quality of the food, i.e., whether the food is compatible with you or not.

Really take some time tasting the food, focus in, and as you chew, get a sense if the food will assimilate with ease or with difficulty. For example, every time I focus in while chewing a carrot, the idea that springs into my mind is, "I am chewing a woody substance. This won't necessarily assimilate but will act as a fibrous 'brush' in my body and help me cleanse." When I focus on chewing rice, I experience that it will "become" part of my body and additionally help me feel grounded. It only takes a little practice, and then you can enjoy having your own experiences with "intuiting" your food.

6. Eat with the Rhythm of the Day

As mentioned earlier, this "digestive-fire" energy called "Pitta" is considered to be manifested in the digestive enzymes produced by the pancreas and secreted into the small intestine where digestion takes place. This area is considered to be the *kosht* (home) of Pitta energy.

This takes place in an area of the abdomen commonly referred to as the celiac plexus. It is also known as the solar plexus because the network of nerve fibers located there under the stomach anatomically radiates outward like rays of the sun, and the function of these nerve fibers is to innervate the abdominal organs.

Indeed, note the poetry of the body, because this solar plexus also refers to the anatomical location in the body where digestion takes place using the energy of heat and fire. Therefore, Ayurvedic thinking recommends that our eating pattern follow a crescendo/decrescendo pattern like the sun. We awaken after the nightly fast of about twelve hours and break the fast with a "breakfast" of moderation. At noon, our solar digestive power is at its zenith, and we partake of the largest meal of the day. In the evening, as our digestive energy wanes, we partake of a correspondingly smaller meal because with less light left in the evening, our body/mind is shifting to prepare us for a less physical and more emotional/spiritual evening job description such as family time, writing, reading, contemplation, or spiritual study. Try this pattern and see how it fits for your body/mind.

7. Avoid Reading, Watching TV, or Exercising during Eating

As was stated earlier in chapter 6, Pitta is involved in the health of the skin, eye, and circulatory system as well as digestion. Therefore it makes good sense not to dilute this energy required for digestion by doing any activity that would drain the digestive fire, such as watching TV or reading during the meal, because these activities involve using your eyes.

My teacher told me that in India, after the meal, people would take some cool water and with eyes closed, gently dab the cool water on their eyelids. This action served as a reminder to "cool down" their Pitta required in vision, thereby not allowing it to compete with the Pitta in the solar plexus doing its job of digestion. In addition, it also makes good sense not to exercise while eating, which would siphon off Pitta to the circulatory system.

For some people, it may be difficult to eat and digest food without reading or watching TV or becoming engrossed in a conversation with someone else because "just eating" is lonely or boring, or they have the gnawing feeling that it's not a good use of their time, as they may need to "get things done." If this is the case, I recommend you begin with a small step. Take one minute to avoid eye contact with the outside world and be with yourself as you eat. One by one, add in the other principles as you can during that minute. Then add another minute, conserving your vision and helping your digestion. Slowly but surely, you will begin to enjoy your process of eating and digestion and feel nourished. You will also feel this is a sanctified time for you to replenish yourself physically as well as spiritually. This is one way of loving yourself.

8. Allow the Food to Nurture You

This may sound silly to say, but food and eating are meant to nourish us. For many people, the process of eating has become robotic and disconnected from a sense of self-nourishment. Why? I think because as stated above, we hurriedly gulp the food down as we excitedly talk to the person next to us or become absorbed in watching TV or reading the paper or, if alone, become lost in the thoughts of the day. In either case, we then look at the empty plate in astonishment. We do have a vague recollection of eating but nevertheless wonder how all that food disappeared from the plate! Therefore, I have another suggestion. Remember that food is meant to nourish our body/mind and give us energy so that we can live in the world and fulfill our unique purpose that life has in store for us. With this in mind, as you eat, think to yourself that this food is nourishing your body and your soul.

9. Allow Five Minutes for Digestion in Quietude

At the beginning of my training in holistic medicine, my wife and I stayed in the Combined Therapy Program at the Himalayan Institute in Honesdale, Pennsylvania. An important part of the program involved eating three meals a day alone in our individual rooms. What? No socialization! Three organized meals a day? And that wasn't all. Part of our training was for us to experience the food in the many ways mentioned above.

What was really foreign to me at the time was to sit alone after the meal was over and focus on digesting the meal. That was quite a revelation. I remember sitting with the feeling of food in my stomach and hearing digestive noises for the first time in my life. How could this be that I had never experienced this before? Well, I reasoned, I'm not talking to someone, I'm not doing something, and I'm not sleeping—rather, I'm awake and paying attention to my body after this meal. That was really a new way of being in the world, and after three meals a day for fourteen days, I never forgot the experience.

I suggest that you try to spend five minutes after your meal with yourself and allow for your own personal experience of digestion and assimilation. If this is too difficult, try one minute. You will be surprised how this and all the above suggestions change your experience of eating for the better.

8

Food for Health and Wellness

I'D LIKE TO share with you the wonderful opportunity I see for the use of foods in healing and preventive medicine. In my practice of medicine and during lectures, I am pleasantly surprised at people's interest in information that is available about food. There is so much information available now and so many opinions that it is easy to become confused about what is right for you.

Some of the popular discussions include flesh foods versus vegetarian, raw food versus cooked food, high fat versus low fat, high carbs versus low carbs, organic versus nonorganic, gluten-free, dairy-free, pescatarian, fruitarian, South Beach, paleo, Pritikin Diet, and so on. All the choices can be mind-boggling. In order to keep it simple, I will stick to the basics and discuss a few ideas that give you some ability to choose for yourself the right diet for you. Food has a profound effect on your health and well-being.

Sugar

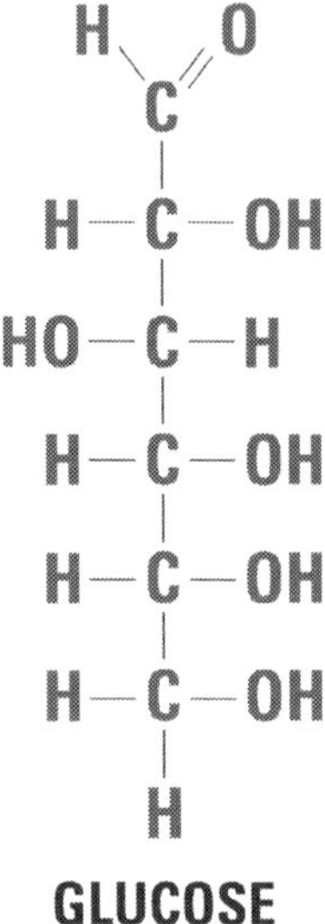

Figure 8-1. Glucose molecule.

Complex versus Simple

I was taught in biochemistry that the cells in our body convert sugar into energy. The chemistry is such that a six-carbon chain of sugar, glucose, (See figure 8-1.) is broken down in a stepwise process inside the cell. The sugar molecule is brought into the cell with the help of insulin and other trace minerals such as chromium and zinc. The end result is that energy is made by the cell for its particular needs. (See figure 8-2.)

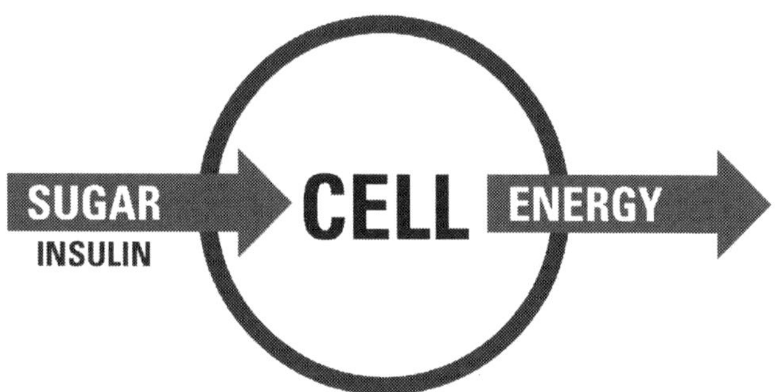

Figure 8-2. Conversion of sugar into energy.

All this sounds good, so why does sugar have such a bad reputation? Now here is the catch. If there are too many individual sugar molecules, called "simple sugars," trying to enter the cell at once, we have a "sugar crisis" on our hands.

Story #1: The Roller-Coaster Ride with Sugar

We need to create a metaphor. Imagine a teacher standing in a classroom surrounded by students. Imagine the classroom represents a cell, and the students all around the classroom represent the sugar molecules that want inside the classroom/cell ASAP. Each student represents an individual sugar molecule. (See figure 8-3.)

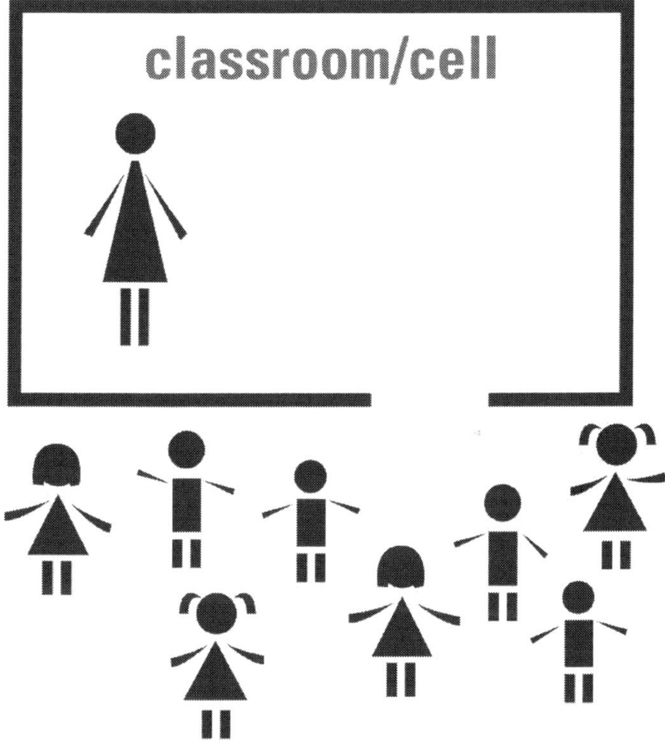

Figure 8-3. Students as unlinked simple sugar molecules about to enter classroom/cell.

Collectively, they represent "simple sugars" found in sugar-laden foods such as candy, soft drinks, stimulant drinks, foods sweetened with high-fructose corn syrup, and so on.

These student/sugar molecules will come toward the classroom/cell, and if enough insulin and trace minerals are present (this is an oversimplified explanation), they will rush inside the cell all at once, creating a massive influx of sugar going into the classroom/cell. (See figure 8-4.)

Figure 8-4. Rapid influx of unlinked sugar into the cell.

During the actual process of digestion, a lot of insulin is needed immediately. The result is that excess insulin is produced by the pancreas and rushed into the bloodstream to push all those individual sugar molecules into the cells all through the body. The cells could be brain, nerve, muscle tissue, or any cells in your body. When this happens, we have a condition where there is too little sugar remaining in the bloodstream. This condition is called "hypoglycemia" and affects all the cells in the body but especially the brain and may be accompanied by symptoms such as tremor, sweating, weakness, dizziness, hunger, confusion, and anxiety as the body hunts for ways to replenish the blood with sugar.

At this point, feeling these symptoms or a sense of uneasiness or craving, the person may reach for sweet food or a drink loaded with simple sugars and becomes temporarily satisfied with the taste of sweet.

Once again, as the new massive supply of simple sugars enters the bloodstream, it creates a temporary hyperglycemia (too much sugar in the bloodstream), which signals the body to call for a massive insulin response, which in turn creates another episode of hypoglycemia with its symptoms of shakiness, uneasiness, or tremor, which in turn causes the person again to reach for something sweet to eat or drink. This whole roller-coaster cycle may repeat itself over and over and sometimes all day long. Sounds familiar?

Sugar Notes

1. Sweeteners including glucose, fructose, sucrose, and grape concentrate are consumed at alarming rates. For years, the average US consumption of sugar was quoted as being anywhere from 100 to 150 pounds per person, per year, as compared with residents in the 1800s who consumed twelve pounds per year. Recently, that number has dropped.[1] (Can you believe that eleven teaspoons of sugar are allegedly in one twelve-ounce can of Coke?)
2. A study showed that the oral intake of 100 grams of sugar in the form of glucose, fructose, sucrose, honey, or orange juice all reduced the body's white blood cells' ability to engulf and destroy bacteria by 50 percent! This began within less than thirty minutes after ingestion and lasted for over five hours.[2]

Considering the above "Sugar Notes," the inescapable conclusion is that many Americans have chronically depressed immune systems. Now back to the story.

Story #2: Sugar Is Absorbed Evenly

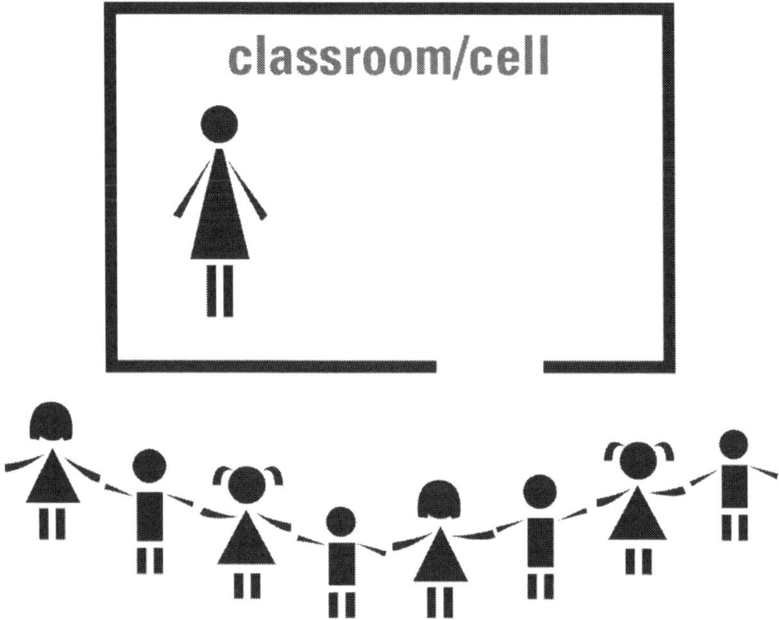

Figure 8-5. Students as linked complex sugars.

Your cell receives sugar evenly—the case for complex sugars. The teacher is back in the classroom/cell, but now all the student/sugar molecules outside the classroom/cell are holding hands. (See figure 8-5.)

This is key. Now as they try to come up and enter the classroom/cell, they must release their handclasp one by one. This allows them to enter the cell in a deliberate and even manner, using insulin and trace minerals more slowly. (See figure 8-6.)

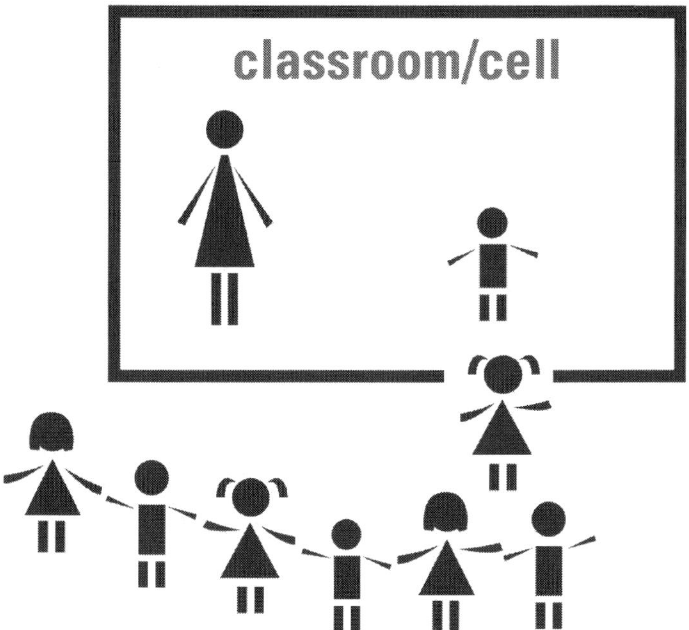

Figure 8-6. Complex sugars entering the cell slower.

This is the story of "complex sugars," which are called "complex carbohydrates": sugar molecules that are naturally connected to each other and only disconnect as needed to provide us with energy in a smooth and even way. This avoids stressing the pancreas, which produces insulin, and avoids using up our trace-mineral reserves before they can be replenished.

Epidemic of Prediabetes

Insulin is getting a lot of press lately. Many of us apparently are walking around with chronic insulin elevations due to our excessive sugar intake. This is because the insulin receptors have been exposed to the roller coaster of elevated sugar levels in the blood for so long (from eating sweets and sweetened foods) that they lose their sensitivity to insulin and no longer work properly; therefore, you need more insulin from the pancreas to help the sugar get into the cell. This is called "insulin resistance," "metabolic syndrome," or "prediabetes."

Since sugar is not permanently high in the blood, there is no diagnosis of diabetes yet. However, the elevated levels of insulin in the blood produced by the pancreas have the following negative effects on the body: This situation promotes chronic inflammation such as sinusitis, arthritis, hypertension, and possibly Alzheimer's disease. It promotes dyslipidemia, a situation where the "bad" clot-promoting fats, LDL and triglycerides, go up, and the "good" protective fats, HDL, go down. It promotes cellular growth in the body and currently is associated with cancers of the colon, liver, and pancreas.[3]

Metabolic syndrome is also associated with cardiovascular disease, diabetes, and nonalcoholic fatty liver disease.[4] At the time of this writing, it is speculated that as much as one-third of the US population may have it. How do you know if you have it? The symptoms include increased abdominal fat, pear-shaped body (when your waist to hip ratio is greater than 1.0 in men or greater than 0.8 in women) accompanied by lab work that shows increased fasting blood sugar, increased triglycerides, and decreased HDL. Little wonder that chronic sinusitis, arthritis, and hypertension with a susceptibility to Alzheimer's disease, heart disease, and cancer are all on the rise in this country. Therefore, one way to avoid these diseases and avoid the highs and lows of the sugar roller coaster is by avoiding simple sugar products, avoiding high-glycemic foods, and examining what's left to eat!

Glycemic Index/Glycemic Load to Our Rescue

The glycemic index (GI) is a measure of how quickly a food shows up as sugar in your bloodstream. The higher the number, the faster that food turns to sugar in your bloodstream. A GI above 70 is considered high, and below 50 is considered low. For example, instant cooked rice is 87, whereas pearled barley is 25. That's quite a difference!

In addition, there is another tool you can use, called "glycemic load" (GL). The GL takes into consideration how much of the specific food a person can typically eat at one sitting. For example, instant cooked rice has a GL of 33, and boiled pearled barley has a GL of 4.

In some foods, the GI of the food may be elevated, but the GL of the food may be low. Take watermelon, for example. The GI is 72, but the GL is only 6. Barry Groves, in his book *Natural Health and Weight Loss*, recommends that we keep the GL of our foods below 15 per meal.[5] The values for the foods stated here come from tables in his book, and I recommend his book for his fine discussion on this topic.

Eat Complex Carbohydrates

Complex carbohydrates, as depicted in the above story, are sugar molecules that are naturally connected together. During digestion, the body must break these molecules apart and feed them to the cell. This takes time and allows a more even and slow requirement for insulin, thereby avoiding the sugar roller coaster mentioned above. Sources of complex carbohydrates include grains such as breads, rice, spelt, buckwheat, oats, rye, and others such as millet, barley, couscous, and quinoa.

If you are diabetic, avoid rice, wheat, and grains in general, because even though they are complex sugars, they are metabolized as higher glycemic-index foods. If you must use a grain and diabetes or weight loss is an issue, use pearled barley, millet, bulgur, or couscous because the glycemic-load values of these grains are 4, 8, 10, and 12, respectively—all below 15.

Whole Grains versus Refined Grains

I suggest you use a whole grain. What does this mean? The "whole" part of "whole grain" refers to the rice or spelt or wheat that is not processed by cutting off the germ and bran in the processing, which is called "refining." Why refine the grain? Cutting off the germ and bran helps preserve the food because we are removing that part of the grain that is perishable and that contains vitamins. The food industry did this so that bacteria can't grow. But then you ask, how do we grow?

The bran is pure fiber, and removing it gives the food a lighter texture, which some people desire, but then we give away all the health-promoting functions associated with fiber. Whole grains are "whole" because they retain their germ and bran so that you are eating the natural vitamins and fiber that nature intended you to have with this particular food. Try it, and see how you feel with whole grains added to your daily meal plan. Here are some ways to work them into breakfast, lunch, and dinner.

Breakfast Suggestions for Grains

Hot cereals such as oatmeal, cream of rice (made by blending rice grains while dry and uncooked and then adding water and cooking until soft), or buckwheat groats are very tasty if used with spices, and they feel hearty in winter.

You can find whole-grain cereals made from wheat, corn, kasha (buckwheat), and rice.

Whole-wheat, rye, or spelt breads and bagels are filling and healthy, and their flours can be made into pancakes.

Dried grains in the form of granola usually have a mixture of oats, nuts, and seeds and may have some dried fruit mixed in for taste and sweetness. They have the advantage of combining grain with fat and protein from the nuts and seeds, which lowers the glycemic index of the meal.

Lunch and Dinner Grain Suggestions

Dinner grains can include brown rice, basmati rice, couscous, millet, and whole-noodle pastas made from wheat, buckwheat (soba), brown rice, and any other whole grain.

Dinner is lighter with whole-grain breads, barley soups, or any of the above if you do not mind digesting these grains late in the day.

Gluten Allergy/Sensitivity

For many people, the protein known as gluten found in wheat, rye, barley, oats, and spelt creates problems. There exists a spectrum of symptoms. On one hand, celiac disease is the condition where the ingestion of gluten will causes severe inflammation in the bowel, along with other harmful symptoms. On the other hand, you may be "sensitive" to gluten and react in a delayed manner with miscellaneous inflammatory symptoms, headaches, problems in the central nervous system, and mood disorders such as depression, to name a few.

Gluten is also being associated with autoimmune disorders such as Hashimoto's thyroiditis. There are blood tests for celiac disease and gluten sensitivities. In my case, my blood studies were normal even though I always felt worse after having ingested wheat. Use your personal experience and act accordingly. If you like oats, you may be able to find oats that have not been exposed to gluten in the shipping and storage process. Thankfully, at this time, gluten-free foods are easy to find in markets, and additionally, restaurants usually have several gluten-free choices on their menus.

How to Drop the Glycemic Index of a Meal

As stated above, if low-glycemic grains are desired, use pearled barley, millet, bulgur wheat, or couscous, as they have a low glycemic-load value. You can also "hide" the sugar by adding good fats, protein, and fiber in the meal. How does this hide or slow down the time it takes for sugar to enter cells?

Fats and protein provide alternative energy sources for our cells, and fat metabolism does not require insulin! In addition, the fiber that accompanies the protein, the fat in nuts, and the sugars in fruit help slow down sugar uptake and therefore help our goal of a slow, even sugar metabolism. In general, grains are well tolerated by most people, and I always feel satisfied (not full) after eating a whole grain. But I can hear you ask, "What goes into the oatmeal or on top of that whole-grain bread or complements the rice/millet/couscous?" The answer is proteins and fats of your choice, of course. Let's see if we can figure out what choices to make in that regard.

Proteins

It may come as a surprise, but protein is not the ideal fuel because it is more difficult for the body to break down protein molecules for energy than it does for sugar molecules. Protein is used by the body to make structures such as cartilage, muscle, and tendons, as well as enzymes that help our cells to make antibodies that fight off bacteria and viruses. Lastly, in starvation, when the body has used up its sugar and fat reserves, it will begin to strip away the muscle, using protein for fuel in its search for an energy source. Let's discuss the different sources of protein and some of their advantages and disadvantages.

Vegetarian Sources of Protein

Grains and Legumes Make a Complete Protein

Protein is formed from chemical building blocks called "amino acids." Legumes such as beans and peas are high in amino acid content. They work especially well when combined with a grain because the amino acids in the grain and legume complement each other to provide all the building blocks necessary to make any protein. That's why we see people from all over the world combining these foods in such dishes as chickpeas (hummus) and pita bread (wheat) in Asia, or tofu (soybeans) and rice in Japan, or lentils and basmati rice in India, or red beans and rice in the southern United States. Many vegetarian diets are built around this foundation of legumes and grains providing protein and carbohydrates as a healthy alternative to flesh consumption.

Other Advantages

There are other reasons for the worldwide daily consumption of beans and peas such as lentils, chickpeas, red beans, split peas, and lima beans, etc.: they are low in cost, low in fat, low in toxicity, high in fiber, high in protein content, and high in life energy. They also help prevent cancer, heart disease, and osteoporosis.

Low in Cost

As of this writing, this is what I found when comparing sources of protein: a five-pound bag of lentils, $4; a five-pound piece of fish, $40 to $60; five pounds of chicken, $30; five pounds of turkey, $30; or ground round, $25. As you can see, vegetarian protein appears to be a less expensive alternative than flesh sources.

Low in Fat

Good fats are absolutely necessary for health. I love and recommend them to my patients, and we will discuss them in some detail later in this chapter. For those people needing less fat, examine the fat content by calories, and you will find that these little gems of food contain 5 to 10 percent fat versus our other sources that contain upward of 30 to 60 percent fat.

Legumes also help regulate our cholesterol production. Bile made in your liver and stored in your gall bladder is secreted into the gut to help you digest the fat in the food you have just eaten. The fat is broken down into cholesterol esters, which are fatty compounds that the body reabsorbs to resynthesize cholesterol. Nature has supplied its own method of reducing cholesterol. How?

Beans and peas have the type of fiber that contains plant sterols—plant chemicals that compete with the cholesterol esters in the gut. When this happens, the body absorbs the plant sterols instead of the cholesterol esters, which then harmlessly pass out in the stool. Now the liver cannot make as much cholesterol as before because its raw materials have passed out of the body! More about this subject will appear later in the book.

High in Fiber

Beans, peas, and legumes are high in fiber. Fiber in food benefits us in many ways. It helps slow down the breakdown and absorption of sugar in our meal, thus helping us to avoid the spikes in sugar absorption we spoke of before. Fiber provides bulk in the intestine, which serves to decrease the time it takes for digestive waste to pass through your body, thus avoiding constipation. The fiber acts like a natural fibrous brush combining with toxic materials and pulling them out into the stool. Fiber has been associated with avoiding stroke and heart disease and may help with gallstone prevention.

Cancer Prevention

Isoflavones, which are compounds in peas and beans, may protect women from breast cancer similar to the way that estrogen-blocking drugs work. These Isoflavones are considered weakly estrogenic and are called "phytoestrogens" (plant estrogens) and bind to estrogen-receptor sites on breast cells. Once bound to the site, they block stronger estrogens and estrogen-like substances from stimulating the cell. Why is that important?

In our environment, there are toxic chemicals (xenobiotics) that are similar to estrogen in their chemical structure and may act like estrogens in stimulating growth of breast tissue. Also, it has been the practice of the dairy industry to fatten up cows by giving them hormones, including estrogen, which then find their way into our bodies. Perhaps this is why there is less breast cancer among the Eastern populations that consume fermented soy products as a major source of protein.

Beware of soy protein isolates and processed soy, as they are considered to be thyroid depressing and enzyme inhibiting, and they form phytic acid in your gut, which combines with minerals, blocking their absorption and causing their elimination in the stool. Surprised? It's true. Unfortunately, when you eat soy, know that your zinc, calcium, and magnesium are eliminated as mineral phytates in the stool!

Live Food/Dead Food

What would you find if you took a piece of beef, fish, or chicken and placed it on the ground and returned after a few days? You might find it full of bacteria and other agents of putrefaction. What would you find if you took a bean or pea or buckwheat groat and placed it outside as before? Now you might find a plant sprouting and expressing life! Why? Because its energy is of a higher state we call "live."

Recently, this concept has been popularized by the raw-food movement in which sprouting or soaking seeds, nuts, legumes, and grains is stressed as an easy way to add live foods to your diet, and I agree. Once you get the right equipment, it's fairly easy, for example, to soak buckwheat groats for an energizing live (uncooked) grain or to sprout red clover or mung beans and add these sprouts to a salad as a live-energy infusion.

For thousands of years, Ayurvedic medicine taught that energy in food can be described as fresh and light (*sattvic*), excitatory and stimulating (*rajasic*), or stale and inert (*tamasic*). Taste the difference between frozen and fresh orange juice. Your taste buds will give the nod to the fresh, real thing. But why? The vitamins, minerals, and calorie content are probably the same. What is it that explains the obvious fact everybody knows that fresh whole foods taste better? It's the concept of energy—life energy—and some foods have more of it than others. Dried beans, seeds, peas, grains, and sprouts are considered alive and are storehouses of life energy waiting to serve you. Nuts such as walnuts or almonds and seeds such as pumpkin seeds can be soaked, dehydrated (under 105°F) and served for days as a protein snack for quick, convenient, and healthy energy.

Some Examples Using Raw Foods

Breakfast

Soaked chia seeds with a teaspoon of coconut oil or some walnuts mixed in
A handful of soaked almonds and fruit such as berries or figs
Raw nut bread[6] with a nut spread and a few blueberries
Soaked buckwheat groats with nuts and some berries of your choice

Lunch

Green salad with the usual mixture of vegetables accompanied by avocado for fat plus soaked and dried pumpkin seeds or walnuts or Brazil nuts or macadamia nuts for protein and additional fat

For a comprehensive discussion concerning live and raw foods, please refer to Dr. Gabriel Cousens's books, *Conscious Eating*[7] or *Rainbow Green Live-Food Cuisine*.

Help Prevent Osteoporosis

As mentioned earlier, isoflavones in beans and peas help protect against breast cancer. An additional benefit may be stronger bones. Ipriflavone, derived from soy, is being marketed as a supplement that helps bone formation. Additionally, we see that legumes are a protein source that provides a more favorable calcium/phosphorus ratio than other protein sources. Why is this important?

Having enough calcium is necessary for bone formation. In medical school, we learned that the kidney would exchange a molecule of calcium for a molecule of phosphorus. It doesn't matter to the kidney which one it excretes into the urine. This is big news for people trying to keep calcium in their bodies because as they ingest phosphorus in their food or supplements, they will automatically lose calcium. Therefore, in people with osteopenia or osteoporosis or with these tendencies, we rarely give supplements with phosphorus in them and counsel them to avoid colas with sequestering agents loaded with phosphorus. I also educate them about the calcium/phosphorus ratio in foods.

Here are a few examples:

- Green leafy vegetables: four molecules of calcium to one molecule of phosphorus—very good

- Beans and peas: one calcium molecule to fifteen phosphorus molecules—neutral
- Flesh foods like chicken: one calcium molecule to thirty molecules of phosphorus—very poor

Flesh and Dairy Sources of Protein

In general, animal protein is a source of complete protein, having all the amino-acid building blocks we have spoken of. In addition, animal fats are our only source of vitamin A (retinol) and vitamin D. Eggs and meat are high in sulfur-containing amino acids, which are important in brain, nervous system, and detoxification functioning. Eggs, as well as all the animal products, are the only usable source of vitamin B_{12} in that there are other kinds of B_{12} in vegetables, but unfortunately, these cannot be assimilated and used by the body. Please refer to *Nourishing Traditions*[8] by Sally Fallon for a complete discussion concerning meat, fish, fowl, eggs, and dairy. She is the living embodiment of Weston Price's work on the healthy use of meats and dairy all over the world, and there are many useful articles on the Weston Price website.

Dairy Products

Milk provides protein, good fats, some sugar, calcium, and B_{12}. For an important discussion about raw milk versus pasteurization, please see Sally Fallon's book, *Nourishing Traditions*, or look on the Weston Price website for articles on the subject.

There are some issues that you need to be careful about before serving milk to your family. Dairy proteins are difficult to digest for many people, and other people are outright lactose intolerant, being unable to make the enzyme lactase that is responsible for breaking down lactose, the sugar in milk. Dairy allergies are common in our population, often responsible for many allergic types of symptoms in children during the first year of life (e.g., skin rashes, ear infections, cramping). Why?

Some people have allergies to casein or whey, the proteins in milk. I find this to be the most common positive result of blood studies for food allergies administered in our clinic. Try boiling the milk and then refrigerating it for later use. Boiling helps break down the proteins for easier digestion, and this may remove symptoms. In addition, please be careful to shop organic and avoid the added growth hormones found in milk from cows that are overproducing milk with high hormone content. There is some evidence that the drop in sperm production in the male population parallels the rise in dairy consumption seen since the 1940s, as excess estrogen may affect the development of male genitalia.[9]

Goat milk has a reputation for being less allergenic, and I have known some families who have successfully used it that way. I personally love raw organic cheeses for a protein and fat source, and they have a glycemic index of zero! Shop organic for the above reasons and to avoid unnecessary additives, oils, and hormones.

Also, cheese protein is high in casein, the protein found in milk that many find allergenic. In addition, if you are sensitive to dairy as a mucus-producing food as discussed in the Ayurvedic section under Kapha, try making *paneer*—the traditional way of making cheese resembling farmer cheese—by bringing milk to a gentle boil, squeezing in the juice of a lemon, and watching the milk curdle. The liquid is whey, and the solids are cheese, called "paneer." After cooling, pour the contents through cheesecloth, squeeze out the whey, refrigerate, and put the solid but light paneer in a container and enjoy its light, ricotta-like flavor. You can drink four to six ounces of whey as a gentle diuretic/kidney cleanser, which also acts to remove mucus from the body. In addition, if you feel allergic to butter, you can learn to make *ghee*, commonly known as clarified butter, in your own kitchen. In the process of making ghee, the milk solids are removed, which renders it less allergenic. For example, even though my personal blood work shows that I am reactive to casein, I do not experience any symptoms when I use ghee.

Eggs

Eggs are considered to be the most complete protein source available. I happen to like eggs as a source for protein and fat, and the glycemic index of eggs is zero. I feel the cholesterol and saturated fat found in eggs are necessary, as we shall see under the discussion about fats. Briefly, the cholesterol found in eggs provides us with a source of pregnenolone, which becomes our hormones DHEA, progesterone, testosterone, and estrogen! Try doing without those!

Did you know that the body uses the cholesterol molecule to make vitamin D when the sun shines on your skin? Vitamin D has a lot of press today for bone health, immune-system support, cancer prevention, insulin regulation, soft-tissue health, and more. Eggs contain vitamin D and vitamin A, which are fat-soluble vitamins. Eggs are an important source of vitamin A called "retinol." Retinol is essential for hormone production and eye health and is a strong antioxidant thought to help with cancer prevention.

Please note that even though we think of leafy green vegetables having plenty of beta-carotene, the precursor to vitamin A, it must be broken down to retinol in the intestines, and then retinol is converted to vitamin A in the liver. It's not actually vitamin A until it gets converted. This is becoming more of a problem in modern society as our livers become more compromised by toxic foods on one hand and stress on the other, so the conversion is becoming more difficult.

Do not buy just any kind of eggs. Eat eggs from chickens that are free to roam and eat plants and insects as part of their natural diet. Another valuable source of vitamins A and D is cod-liver oil. I use it often in my medical practice. The Weston A. Price Foundation suggests that vitamins A and D occur together in an optimal ratio in nature, and that's what we should try for in our diet. Therefore, when supplementing vitamin D for those who have low blood levels of vitamin D, I currently recommend the use of fermented cod-liver oil, which supplies this ratio of vitamins naturally rather than giving vitamin D by itself. Speaking of fish...

Fish

Fish is tasty, is a great protein source, has a zero glycemic index, and can be very beneficial for its healthy fat content, the omega-3 fatty acids, which we will cover later in this chapter. Some examples of fish known for their high omega-3 fat content are sardines, salmon, tuna, and rainbow trout. Unfortunately, the cold-water, deep-sea fish, as well as fish in inland waters, are also exposed to toxic metals such as mercury. This problem is becoming more acknowledged as the Food and Drug Administration, the National Academy of Sciences, and the Environmental Protection Agency are issuing warnings[10] about limiting fish meals in sensitive groups of people such as pregnant mothers (fetus at risk for brain damage), nursing mothers, and young children. Methyl mercury, the type found in these fish, is considered toxic to the nervous system and may induce symptoms such as numbness and tingling in the lips, fingers, and toes; weakness; irritability; headache; salivation; and mental dullness. The smaller and younger fish have less contamination, as will be explained by the food-chain discussion below.

Be careful with nursery or farm-raised fish, which may be fed "wild" fish, in which toxic metals like mercury and arsenic are found. Testing for mercury levels can be done by hair analysis or urine samples. At this time, it appears that Alaskan salmon, anchovies, sardines, and rainbow trout should be safer for ingestion, but it's important to keep up with the current information about toxicity in the area where you live. It's best to avoid fish such as swordfish, shark, king mackerel, and tilefish. Be careful about eating Great Lakes whitefish and fish from other smaller lakes, as contamination from PCBs may be a problem. In general, avoid the large fish that eat smaller fish. Why? The answer lies in understanding how the food chain works.

Understanding the Food Chain

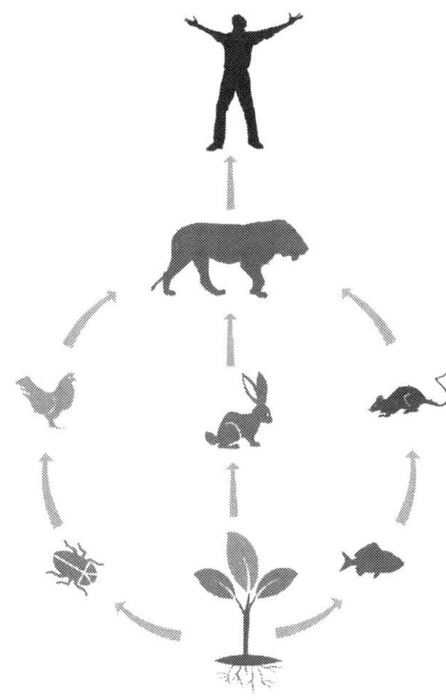

Figure 8-7. The food chain.

I like to think of the food chain as beginning with plants such as grasses growing on the land or algae and other vegetation in the sea. Then a small animal or fish consumes some of these plants. Any pesticides or mercury in those plants now becomes stored in the fatty tissue of the small animal or on the muscle fibers of the fish, as is the case with mercury. Then along comes the next biggest animal or fish that eats several of the smaller animals or fish until it's satisfied. (See figure 8-7.)

All the pesticides or toxic metals in the smaller fish or animals are now in the fatty tissue (liver, marrow) or muscle of the bigger fish or animal. For example, by the time you get to a large fish like tuna, it has consumed a lot of mercury and arsenic and whatever else is stored in all the fat or muscle tissue of all the smaller fish that ate the smaller fish that ate the plants.

This process repeats itself until the "top-gun" predator—man, king of the food chain—eats the beef, fish, or fowl, and thereby consumes food highly concentrated in toxins. Now we can understand how legumes such as split peas, lentils, chickpeas, black-eyed peas, vegetables, or algae, being plants, are on the bottom of the food chain and are, therefore, a protein source comparatively very low in toxic residues.

Chicken, Turkey, and Beef

These can be excellent sources of complete protein and fat, meaning that they have all the amino acids necessary for the body to make protein and, according to Sally Fallon, contain the fat-soluble vitamins A and D necessary to absorb it. These flesh products have a zero glycemic index and thereby satisfy those people who are reducing their sugar intake. I also believe that the saturated fat they supply is healthy and necessary, as will be explained in the discussion on fats. They are a mainstay of the paleo diets we see popular in the media now, which emphasize flesh protein, some fat, nuts, seeds, fruits, and vegetables, and avoid grains, legumes, and simple sugars.

Chicken fat has a history of being medicinal and has been considered healthy for centuries. Turkey has a higher concentration of

L-tryptophan in the meat that brings on relaxation. However, heads up on the following information.

First, as a group, chicken, turkey, and beef contain a lot of phosphorus relative to calcium because chemical energy is stored as a phosphorus compound in the muscle tissue of the animal, which we eat. Therefore, flesh is high in phosphorus and low in calcium. The calcium will be traded off in the kidneys and eliminated in the urine, as mentioned previously, thereby increasing the likelihood of osteoporosis in those who are susceptible to it.

Second, shop organic, in my opinion, unless you're prepared to eat animals that may be raised in unhealthy and overcrowded conditions and fed many "xenobiotics" (foreign substances such as antibiotics, steroids, unhealthy feeds, and pesticides) that accumulate in the fat of the animal and find their way into your body as you digest them. For example, if the cow or steer had been fed growth hormones and steroids to enhance growth characteristics or was fed antibiotics because of weak immunity, it's reasonable to assume that these chemicals are making their way into your body when you eat them. If the chicken has been fed mostly corn and soy, its tissue contains more vegetable oil than if the chicken had grazed on grass and insects. In that case, you're not eating healthy chicken fat; you're eating chicken with a high vegetable-fat content. And speaking of fat, I would like to talk with you about the subject of "good" and "bad" fats.

Fats

I can remember the days when everyone felt "all fats are bad." Nowadays, people realize that there are many helpful fats that can be used for wellness and health.

Omega-6 and Omega-3 Fatty Acids

These fats are termed "essential fatty acids" because they cannot be made by the body and therefore must be ingested in food. As a group, they serve to decrease inflammation, enhance immunity, and may have a positive effect on depression and mood. Sources of omega-3 include walnuts, soybeans, and flaxseeds, as well as eggs and fish. Omega-3 oil in the form of dietary fish or fish oil is very good for your heart. Studies have shown that they can do the following:

1. Lower triglyceride levels
2. Inhibit arteriosclerosis
3. Lower blood pressure
4. Reduce platelet aggregation (like aspirin) and thereby reduce blood clotting
5. Suppress heart arrhythmias and decrease sudden cardiac death

That's a lot of benefit from fish!

Flaxseed Oil

Many people consume flaxseed oil, believing it to have an anti-inflammatory effect on the body. In addition, we do know that flaxseeds have high lignan content. Lignans are fibers found in plants, and they exert a weak estrogenic effect. Plants that have this property are called "phytoestrogens," and they help protect women from breast cancer in the way described above when we spoke about isoflavones. I include one teaspoon a day of flaxseed powder in my breast-cancer prevention recommendation to women. Sources include flaxseeds, nuts, whole grains, legumes, vegetables, and fruits.

Monounsaturated Fats

Did you know that nuts, in moderation, can be very beneficial to your heart? Nuts contain monounsaturated fatty acids (MUFA) and omega-3 polyunsaturated fatty acids (PUFA), mentioned above, that help to lower low-density lipoprotein, LDL, the bad fat that oxidizes easily, causing inflammation, heart disease, lower total cholesterol, and coronary events. Some of these actions by nuts may be due to their natural sources of vitamin E, copper, magnesium, folic acid, and dietary fiber all helping the heart in different ways to function normally.

In addition, research has shown that a handful of mixed nuts eaten every day reduces all causes of mortality by 20 percent![11] Sources include almonds, walnuts, pecans, peanuts (actually a legume), cashews, pistachios, and macadamia nuts. Another famous monounsaturated fat is olive oil. Did you know that it has anticancer properties? Take a look at this information referenced in the discussion that follows about healthy fats such as olive oil.

HEALTHY FATS

Research that looked at more than 60,000 women in Sweden from age 40 to 76 years found that over the course of about 4 years, those who ate the largest proportion of oil from monounsaturated suffered the lowest risk of breast cancer.

According to the researchers, if two women ate the same amount of total fat calories, the one who ate 10 more grams of monounsaturated fat per day cut her chance of breast cancer in half.

50%!!!

Good Fats Help Prevent Cancer

All from monounsaturated fat! Olive oil is a good source of monounsaturated fat, and one tablespoon provides ten grams of fat. Therefore, I include olive oil, avocado, and nuts in my recommendations to women to help them prevent breast cancer because these foods all have monounsaturated fat in them. I think everyone has heard of the benefits of olive oil, but fewer people have heard of the benefits of cholesterol and saturated fats. If not, I have a few surprises in store for you.

Good Fats Help Weight Loss!

One of our research-oriented patients referred me to some reading material about healthy weight-loss ideas. We discussed the idea that a person could lose weight by eating more fat, not less! As unbelievable as it sounds, it's true. By staying off refined sugars, keeping carbohydrates to a reasonable level, and eating healthy, organic, grass-fed saturated-fat products, a person can lose weight and enjoy the process, feel satisfied (not depressed or deprived), and look forward to his or her meals.

"But fats and cholesterol," our minds scream out, and then we ask, "What about weight gain and heart disease?" Well, surprise! It's not what you think! First, the idea that fat and cholesterol can be good actually comes about from scientific studies.

Surprise #1: Oxidation Is the Problem

Dr. Bruce Fife, in his book *Eat Fat, Look Thin*, points out that in the sixty-year period from 1910 to 1970, heart disease went from being rare to the number-one killer it is today.[12] Well, how did we eat during those years? He relates the following:

- The use of animal fat and butter decreased markedly.
- The intake of cholesterol stayed approximately the same.
- The use of vegetable oils in the form of margarine, shortening, and processed oil *increased 400 percent!*

How is it possible that we did not increase our cholesterol intake (actually up 1 percent) all those years, and heart disease goes from nil to the number-one killer?

"Oh, oh," you say.

What about the use of vegetable oil, corn oil, cottonseed oil, safflower oil, soy oil, margarine, and shortening up by 400 percent! Perhaps they were and are the problem. This makes total sense when you consider the chemical structure of those oils. The unsaturated nature of vegetable oil allows it to take in unstable oxygen (termed "oxidation"). You can see this in action when you cut an apple and the part that is exposed to air turns brown. Do you really want to eat the brown part? Of course not, because you can see that it's oxidized, and you instinctively know that something in it is not right. When this happens to polyunsaturated vegetable oil, this rancid, brownish oxidized fat now affects all the food it touches—breaking down cell membranes and affecting the DNA in the cells that it comes in contact with—and does the same thing to your cells when you swallow this now-oxidized food, leading to heart disease, cancer, and symptoms of aging.

Surprise #2: Cholesterol Is Important

The famous and often-quoted Framingham, Massachusetts, heart study, sponsored by the government, studied more than five thousand people over a forty-year period; Dr. Mary Enig and Sally Fallon reported the following:[13]

- Almost half the people with heart attacks had low cholesterol.
- People whose cholesterol had decreased had a higher risk of dying from heart disease and all other causes!

A 1989 study published in the renowned medical journal *Lancet* stated that women with a very low cholesterol level had *five times* the death rate of those women who had "normal" cholesterol.[14]

So what's going on? As it turns out, cholesterol is very important to our normal functioning. According to Dr. Mary Enig and Sally Fallon, who wrote *Eat Fat, Lose Fat*, the cholesterol molecule;

- helps make up the structure of our cell membranes, and saturated fats help to keep these membranes sturdy and actually make up 50 percent of the membrane;
- is the precursor for sex hormones, stress hormones, and DHEA;
- allows the formation of vitamin D in the presence of sunlight and helps bone, nerve, and muscle tissue;
- forms bile salts to help digest fats;
- is rich in mother's milk; and
- acts as an antioxidant to protect us from oxidation-induced cancer and heart disease.

Dr. Fife says it's not the unoxidized cholesterol that is the problem; it's the oxidation (browning)—free-radical activity—caused by vegetable oils and other factors such as overcooking or leaving food such as powdered milk and cheeses out in the air too long.[15] He adds that overly processed foods like bologna or salami may have significant amounts of oxidized cholesterol and recommends they be avoided.

My Recommendations

- I would not recommend cooking with vegetable oils such as canola, peanut, safflower, corn, and soy oil because they are largely polyunsaturated oils.
- I would not use hydrogenated vegetable oils or margarine in any form.
- I would recommend cooking with olive oil at low temperatures or with coconut oil, sesame oil, or clarified butter at regular temperatures because they are more saturated and less likely to become oxidized. Once we are no longer worried about cholesterol that has not been oxidized, then we can move on to discuss the beneficial effects of saturated fats from the coconut plant and grass-fed animal products such as milk, butter, cream, eggs, cheese, chicken, and beef including where to find them and how to use them.

Saturated Fats

Let's take a closer look at saturated fats. As I write this, I'm still astonished that the much-maligned saturated fats (coconut oil, butter, palm-kernel oil, flesh fats) are so helpful in a variety of situations and the polyunsaturated vegetable oils (safflower, sunflower, walnut, corn oil, soybean oil, cottonseed, peanut, and canola) are not so good.

Saturated Fats and Heart Disease

In a study published in the *Journal of Clinical Epidemiology*,[16] Dr. Fife reports that all the research on saturated fats and polyunsaturated fats that related to heart disease showed they found no positive correlation between saturated-fat consumption and heart disease, and in later studies, the conclusions were that saturated fat may indeed be protective!

Along those lines, consider this: Barry Groves, in his book *Natural Health and Weight Loss*, reports that the traditional Inuit (Eskimo) diet as studied in the 1950s was a very low-carbohydrate/high-fat diet, which included whale, salmon, some berries, and some digested stomach content from these animals' stomachs.[17] On this diet, Inuit blood-cholesterol levels were very high, but triglycerides were low, and the Inuit people did not have obesity, coronary heart disease, diabetes, and cancer. I repeat—high cholesterol but no heart disease!

This correlates with what Dr. Barry Sears, author of the *Zone Diet*, reports in his book, *The Anti-Inflammation Zone*. He asserts that focusing on the triglyceride/high-density lipoprotein ratio (TG/HDL) rather than following cholesterol levels is useful and concludes that the TG/HDL ratio is very predictive in forecasting heart disease, diabetes, and diseases of inflammation. According to Dr. Sears, "a 2001 study found that those who had a low TG/HDL ratio, even if they smoked, were sedentary, had high LDL (bad) cholesterol, or hypertension, had half the risk of developing heart disease than those with a high TG/HDL ratio who had no other risk factors for heart disease." Further, he reports "that Harvard Medical School studies showed that patients with a high TG/HDL ratio can be up to sixteen times more likely to suffer a heart attack than those with a low TG/HDL ratio."[18]

Saturated Fats and Cancer

Dr. Fife continues that researchers looked for a link between saturated fat and cancer and found that saturated fat had a protective effect against cancer rather than a causative one when compared with other oils. "*Polyunsaturated oils were identified as causing cancer, and the higher the degree of unsaturation, the greater the risk*" (italics mine).[19]

Saturated Fats and Stroke

Dr. Fife adds that saturated fats help to prevent strokes in both humans and animals. Studies from Japan in the 1980s found a relationship between increased dietary fat and a decrease in death from ischemic stroke in humans. Also, in a twenty-year study at Harvard Medical School involving middle-aged men who participated in the Framingham Heart Study, the conclusion was that saturated fat lowers the rate of stroke, and the highest incidence of stroke was associated with the most polyunsaturated fat intake.[20]

All these authors report that saturated fats have the following benefits:

1. Our cell membranes are largely made up of fats. They require the right fats to maintain the integrity and stiffness of the cell, or else they soften and begin to "leak." Since 50 percent of every cell membrane is saturated fat, cholesterol and other saturated fats are necessary for optimal functioning.
2. Saturated fats support the immune system. An example is lauric acid. This fatty acid is found in coconut oil (and in mother's milk) and is antibacterial, antifungal, and antiviral.
3. Saturated fats help calcium absorption, hence avoiding osteoporosis.
4. Saturated fats help protect the liver from toxic effects of alcohol, drugs, and toxins.
5. Saturated fats have positive effects in many health categories such as energy improvement, weight loss, cancer prevention,

inflammation reduction, and skin health, as well as beneficial effects on the heart (fat is its primary energy source), lungs (surfactant), kidneys (cellular communication), and hormones (cholesterol is the precursor molecule ending up in the production of progesterone, cortisol, DHEA, estrogen, and testosterone).

What Are These Surprisingly Good Fats?

The following percentages were taken from Dr. Fife's book *Eat Fat, Look Thin*.[21]

1. Coconut oil: 92 percent saturated, 6 percent monounsaturated, 2 percent polyunsaturated

   It's well known that the populations in Polynesia and Asia who live on coconut products and oils do not suffer from heart disease, cancer, and degenerative diseases. Dr. Enig reports that coconut oil helps weight loss because it contains medium-chain fatty acids that are metabolized differently and suggests taking one tablespoon ten minutes before eating your meal.[22] There are whole books on the subject, and I suggest you do some reading on them. Since trying coconut oil, I use it for cooking or for melting it on rice or on breads with a little sea salt for a terrific-tasting, healthy snack. I have also used it medicinally for skin health and to improve symptoms from Alzheimer's disease on the theory that medium-chain triglyceride metabolism provides an alternative energy source for the brain. Dr. Fife has written books and articles dedicated to educating us about the use of coconut products.[23] Dr. Mary Newport has written and reported about her positive experience while treating her husband with medium-chain triglycerides for Alzheimer's disease.[24]

2. Butter: 66 percent saturated, 30 percent monounsaturated, 4 percent unsaturated

   For years, my wife and I used clarified butter (ghee) for frying at any temperature because of its great taste and because it oxidizes less during the heating process due to its high degree of saturation and low degree of unsaturation. It is easy to make at home.

   How to make ghee. Take four to eight sticks of unsalted organic butter, preferably from grass-fed cows, and bring them to a minimal boil and let simmer. The hissing sound is the sound of the water boiling out. Once the hissing sound stops, the ghee is finished. Be careful not to burn it by overcooking it. After cooling a bit, skim off the milky portion on the surface. Pour off the liquid golden oil (this is the ghee) into an earthenware or metal container. The milk solids on the bottom may be discarded if you are allergic to casein or milk, or you may eat them separately. The ghee will solidify at room temperature and may be kept in or outside the fridge.

3. Olive oil: 14 percent saturated, 77 percent monounsaturated (mostly monounsaturated), 9 percent polyunsaturated

   Olive oil is a major component of the Mediterranean diet. It helps prevent inflammation, heart disease, hypertension, stroke, and cancer. See the discussion above describing how monounsaturated fats helped prevent breast cancer. In summary, according to the researchers, if two women ate the same amount of total fat calories, the one who ate ten more grams of monounsaturated fat per day cut her chance of breast cancer in half—50 percent![25] This amounts to one tablespoon of olive oil. I use it for low-temperature frying, and it is the oil of choice in all my salads. I recommend using extra-virgin oil, pressed from organic olives and sold in a green bottle that prevents oxidization from sunlight. The taste should have a certain amount of pungency or "bite" in your throat, indicating it's good quality.

4. Flesh sources such as beef /lamb/pork: approximately 52 percent saturated, 44 percent monounsaturated, 3 to 5 percent polyunsaturated

   Please note that this compares to our human body fat (97 percent saturated/monounsaturated with 3 percent polyunsaturated fat). No, I'm not suggesting we eat human fat! I am suggesting that those who live on grass-fed, free-range animal products all over the world in various countries and cultures do very well (live long lives and are able-bodied, etc.) because they consume such small amounts of polyunsaturated oils, and the saturated fats in their diets help protect the unsaturated fats from free-radical oxidation. But be careful and note that if you consume regular flesh, fowl, or poultry that is not grass fed, you actually consume an animal that was probably raised on soy and corn, and its oils are more vegetable-like and therefore more unsaturated and more likely to result in the oxidative free-radical damaging process that we are trying to avoid.

My Own Survey

Even as I write this, I'm still amazed that everything we have been taught through the years does not hold up to the ancient wisdom of the food traditions over the world. Excitedly, I interviewed people at home and at work. Here is what they said:

1. A patient's relatives in Poland who continued with grass-fed chicken, milk, eggs, and fats had no problems with cholesterol, heart disease, or diabetes.
2. Our consultant internist's eyes lit up as he described his family back in Iran, who went for the "fattest parts of the sheep they could find," and all were healthy.
3. Our friend's ninety-two-year-old grandmother, who lives in the mountains of Romania and tends to her cows and chickens, is able-bodied and independent and living on the high-saturated fatty foods of her grass-fed animals. She states that when the people leave the mountains and go to the cities, they eat differently (processed food, hydrogenated vegetable oils, sugar, etc.) and come down with diseases like diabetes, heart disease, or cancer.

In Summary

I recommend everything in moderation. Please take a close look at your diet and consider removing the unhealthy fats in your life by doing the following:

- Cook with a stable oil that will not oxidize during the heating process, such as coconut oil, ghee, or beef fat. Olive oil is popular but should be limited to low temperature usage. The polyunsaturated oils will likely become oxidized during cooking or exposure to open air and then oxidize any foodstuffs that they come into contact with.

- Read labels carefully. When you find polyunsaturated oils such as safflower or sunflower or canola or cottonseed oil added to bars or chips, think of these oils contaminating their neighboring foods by beginning the oxidation process, thus bringing us down the road to inflammatory diseases such as heart disease, cancer, and age-related degenerative changes.
- Consider the evidence that cholesterol is not the villain and is needed, since it is necessary for vitamin D, hormone synthesis, bile formation, and cell-membrane structure, and discuss this with your doctor.
- Consider the evidence that high triglycerides caused by sugar intake may be a more accurate predictor for heart disease, and ask your doctor to study your triglyceride to HDL ratio with you.
- Read, research, and experiment with your diet, and enjoy the process!

Unhealthy Fats

Arachidonic Acid or Not

There are some fats I would avoid. Some researchers such as Dr. Barry Sears feel that foods high in the fatty acid arachidonic acid have the effect of stimulating a specific set of hormones in our bodies called "prostaglandins series 2" that induce an allergic response, promote inflammation, and suppress our immune functioning.[26] Milk, meat, butter, and eggs are high in these fats and are best avoided if you suffer with inflammatory problems such as arthritis, eczema, sinusitis, ear infections, heart disease, or allergies. On the other hand, noted author and food researcher Sally Fallon of the Weston A. Price Foundation feels that this fatty acid is very important for health and recommends the consumption of meat, whole milk, butter, and eggs from grass-fed animals on organic soils.[27]

Trans Fats

The processing of oil by hydrogenation is a process whereby hydrogen molecules are bubbled into fat in order to make the oil softer at room temperature. This creates unnatural fats known as trans-fatty acids. Examples are margarine and hydrogenated cottonseed oil. These fats are stickier than normal fats (you can taste the gummy quality in your mouth) and may cause fatty deposits in blood vessels and other organs. Their unnatural shape has an effect on how cells function. Hydrogenated oils also raise LDL cholesterol (the bad one linked to heart disease), lower the protective HDL (good cholesterol), and may be linked to certain cancers. Read labels and avoid hydrogenated fats such as hydrogenated palm, soybean, and cottonseed oils often found in chips, cakes, frostings, cookies, desserts, artificial cheeses, margarine, and shortening.

Free Radicals

Have you heard the term "free radicals"? Polyunsaturated fats such as corn oil and other vegetable oils with a high degree of unsaturation are best avoided because their unsaturated state quickly fills up with oxygen molecules—the oxidation we spoke about when we talked about free radicals. Fats and oils may become oxidized under high heat during the frying process. Oxygen combines with these oils in an unstable way and oxidizes or burns the oil not unlike a slice of apple left open on the table turns brown or a pat of butter left open and exposed to air turns yellow. These food molecules are newly created during the frying process and are termed "free radicals."

They are unstable molecules because they chemically hunger to become attached to another molecule. Once ingested, they chemically invade other food molecules, and once inside your body, they can damage whatever cells they can grab on to. It appears they are responsible for many diseases associated with oxidation, such as heart disease, cancer, and diseases of aging. Therefore, cooking with these oils or eating foods prepared with them are likely to result in eating damaged food with negative results on your body. Avoid oils such as corn, safflower, soy, sunflower, and canola oils. My preference at this time is to use fats and oils that resist this oxidation process, such as sesame oil, the monounsaturated fat olive oil, and the saturated fats such as butter, clarified butter (ghee), and coconut oil.

As we spoke about above, it seems like common sense not to eat the apple where it browned or the butter where it yellowed. Even if we didn't know anything about oxidation, our intuition springs to life and exclaims, "Avoid those discolored foods." The colorful fruits and veggies we see all around us help us stay healthy and protect us from illness. Let's examine a few examples.

Fruits and vegetables

Fruits and vegetables serve to protect us in many ways.

Osteoporosis

Green leafy vegetables are loaded with calcium, and their calcium-to-phosphorus ratio is actually close to 4:1. This means that when you eat broccoli, kale, spinach, or romaine lettuce, you're obtaining three to four parts calcium for every one part phosphorus—as opposed to the other way around—thirty to forty parts phosphorus to one part calcium when we eat chicken, turkey, beef, and the like. Remember, the kidney exchanges one part calcium for one part phosphorus, so the more phosphorus in our diets, the greater potential for eliminating the much-needed calcium for our bones.

Cancer Prevention

Lycopene is a carotenoid that provides the red color in tomatoes and other fruits. This pigment helps prevent prostate cancer, and lycopene supplements have been used in the treatment of prostate cancer. Therefore, I advise men to frequently eat red grapefruit, red apricots, tomatoes, tomato paste, or watermelon for prostate health. Lycopene is best absorbed with a little fat; therefore, I always take my tomatoes in a salad with a little olive oil. For men with prostate problems, I may recommend a teaspoon of tomato paste with a few drops of olive oil mixed in.

Indole-3-carbinol, the enzyme found in the brassica species of vegetables (broccoli, kale, brussels sprouts, cauliflower, collard greens, arugula), helps protect against breast cancer in three ways:

- It deactivates estrogen, so there is less estrogen in our bodies to stimulate the breast-cell estrogen-receptor sites that make the cells grow.

- It induces liver detoxification, which in turn helps destroy chemicals that are potentially carcinogenic.
- It increases apoptosis—the name given for programmed cell death. Our cells have a built-in mechanism for destroying themselves under the right conditions so that new healthy cells can take their place—in cancer, this mechanism does not work properly, and cells try to live forever.

All that from broccoli!

Medicinal mushrooms such as *maitake* and *reishi* have been used in the treatment of cancer. They activate natural killer cells (that part of the immune system responsible for destroying cancer cells), are antiproliferative (when cancer cells are growing rapidly), and help protect normal cells against the toxicity of chemotherapy.

Heart Disease

Taking an apple a day is probably a good idea. Here is one reason. Behold, an apple is loaded with the soluble fiber pectin, a carbohydrate chain capable of dissolving in water. Pectin solidifies at lower temperatures and is used in jams and jellies. If you are trying to reduce cholesterol naturally, the pectin in fruits and vegetables helps this goal by combining with the bile acids (made by the liver, stored in the gall bladder, and secreted into the gut to help digest fats in our diet) in the gut and escorting them out of the body as fecal fats in our waste. This reduces the amount of bile acids that can be reabsorbed from the gut to form new cholesterol. Studies have shown that eating fruits and vegetables high in pectinaceous fiber have increased fecal-fat excretion by 30 to 40 percent![28] Foods containing pectin include apples, citrus fruits, carrots, and beans.

Potpourri

Onions and Garlic

They have sulfhydryl groups that chemically help to form glutathione, a compound that removes heavy metals such as mercury and arsenic from our cells.

Carrots and Green Vegetables

Foods such as spinach, broccoli, and collards are rich in beta-carotene, one of the dietary carotenoids. Beta-carotene is a potent antioxidant and may help in a variety of ways such as cancer protection and protection against heart disease. Other dietary carotenoids called "lutein" and "zeaxanthin" help in the prevention of cataracts and macular degeneration. They are yellow to red pigments found in corn and green vegetables such as green beans, peas, brussels sprouts, cabbage, kale, collards, spinach, and lettuce and are also found in fruits such as kiwi and honeydew.

Blueberries, Blackberries, and Cherries

These are filled with bioflavonoids that give them their blue-red color. They are beneficial for the prevention and treatment of varicose veins. Their antioxidant power should help with conditions affected by oxidation such as heart disease, cancer, and premature aging of the skin.

Grapes

Red grape skins offer us resveratrol, a plant-based flavonoid showing anti- atherosclerotic activity, along with immune-stimulating and anticancer effects.

Spices

They help our health as well as our taste buds. Take turmeric (the yellow spice), for example. Turmeric contains curcumin, a phytochemical capable of inhibiting inflammation and having a positive effect on the initiation, promotion, and proliferation stages of cancer. Turmeric is often the main ingredient in anti-inflammatory supplements that people use to reduce inflammation associated with injury or the pain of arthritis. In those situations, I may begin treatment by prescribing turmeric capsules instead of using the traditional nonsteroidal anti-inflammatory meds (NSAIDs).

Considering Ayurveda, turmeric stimulates Vata (see chapter 6 and chapter 9) and is applied to balance earth and fire when they are too strong in an individual. Bitter is said to enhance the liver's digestive functioning, and turmeric is considered a digestive bitter. For wellness, I was taught to make a masala consisting of turmeric, cumin, and coriander browned in a little ghee, known as clarified butter. I also use olive oil or coconut oil for this purpose. You can use this sauce to brown onions, spread it on a piece of bread, or use as a sauce for rice, etc. I believe that turmeric is one of our helpers that will be shown to help prevent Alzheimer's disease because of its anti-inflammatory effect.

Salt

Let's not forget this wonderful spice that helps stimulate digestion, helps our nervous system, and provides many of our needed trace minerals. I am indebted to Dr. Brownstein and his wonderful little book *Salt Your Way to Health.*[29] I have gotten over my "salt phobia" and use it daily. Importantly, he states that processed salt does not provide these needed trace minerals. Only sea salt does.

Water

By now, everyone knows that you have to stay hydrated for good health for many reasons. At any given time, our body/brain is 50 to 75 percent water. We are water beings! The recommendation is to drink one-half your body weight in ounces.

Let's figure this out for the typical 70-kilogram person. Seventy multiplied by 2.2 equals 154 pounds divided by 2 equals 77 ounces, which is approximately 9 glasses of water a day if you are 154 pounds. Figure up or down, depending on your weight and activity.

According to the wonderful book *Your Body's Cry for Water*,[30] you must figure that coffee, soft drinks, and tea all cause a deficiency in hydration. So for every cup of coffee or tea, you have to add an additional glass of water to be fully hydrated! Wow. Nevertheless, relax and experiment and see how you feel by consciously hydrating yourself daily. Remember, our needs are very individualistic. Therefore, if we apply our mindfulness to our own personal situation, it will help us use this information to feel fulfilled and healthy.

I've mentioned a few of our delightful and colorful veggies, fruits, and spices along with our more commonplace salt and water to stimulate your interest and awe for their health benefits. For the most part, you can take advantage of our knowledge of foods to eat naturally and be healthy. In addition to what nature provides, I do believe there are times in our lives such as specific ages, developmental periods, and situations such as illness, injury, or wellness maintenance when we need specific supplementation to lend us a healing hand. This includes vitamins and minerals.

Vitamins and Minerals, Our Temporary Helpers

In my medical practice, I see people taking too many or too few supplements. Why? I think it's because people are confused about how and why to use them. I'd like to give you a few guidelines that I find useful.

First, buy them from someone who has done the research about quality, quantity, and indication. Second, use them when you need them, and stop when they are no longer helping. Third, supplements are usually best taken with food unless otherwise stated. Now let's look at some common situations that call for supplementation.

Smoking Cigarettes

I try to protect the person from the oxidation byproducts of smoke by recommending the antioxidant vitamins A, C, E, and the mineral selenium. I also give milk thistle to help protect the liver while the liver is performing its detoxification function.

PMS

Many symptoms such as mood swings, anxiety, depression, irritability, and insomnia are often due to excess estrogen and may respond to a supplement program that addresses this issue. I like to place a woman on a protocol for ten days leading up to her menses that includes dietary advice that reduces her intake of estrogenic foods, and I add B_6 and magnesium, which help the metabolism of estrogen in the liver.

Osteoporosis Prevention

During the perimenopausal period of a woman's life, it is essential to minimize bone loss and try to reduce it from 2 percent a year to 1 percent or 0 percent, if possible. I recommend a diet that utilizes the calcium-to-phosphorus ratio as discussed above to increase the absorption of available calcium, and I suggest weight-bearing exercise and a calcium supplement that is more likely to be absorbed, such as calcium citrate or calcium glycinate in combination with magnesium. I make a similar recommendation to the elderly. Take your calcium in the evening because it's been shown that we lose most of our bone during periods of inactivity such as during sleep.

Prostate Health

Zinc and vitamin B_6 are important supplements for the prostate gland because they help keep the level of the hormone prolactin down, which in turn helps regulate the hormone dihydrotestosterone, the hormone responsible for prostate cell growth. Pumpkin seeds are a natural source of zinc and B_6.

Heart Health

A simple four-part plan for the prevention and treatment of heart disease using supplements (to list just a few as an example) might consist of the following:

1. Reducing cholesterol (not my favorite idea—see above in fats discussion) with niacin, lecithin, and garlic

2. Preventing the oxidation of the "bad" cholesterol by using antioxidant vitamins A, E, and C and the trace mineral selenium
3. Preventing the inflammatory process that results in damage to the arterial wall with fish oil and turmeric capsules
4. Inhibiting the blood-clotting process with vitamin E, fish oil, garlic, and magnesium

We have briefly reviewed some suggestions concerning healthy sugars, proteins, fats, vegetables, and fruits and the use of supplements with an eye toward disease prevention. Good health also involves avoiding what is harmful. Therefore, let's take a look at some foods best avoided in order to remain healthy.

Foods to Avoid

Xenobiotics

These are biologically active materials in our food that may act as environmental toxins and enter the body, such as preservatives, pesticides, herbicides, fertilizers, toxic metals, hormones, colorings, and antibiotics. For example, we know that many of these xenobiotics may be carcinogenic in that they act like strong estrogens stimulating estrogen-receptor sites on breast cells and possibly contributing to the rise in breast cancer. Not good!

An example is milk, depending on its source. We spoke previously of the increased intake of dairy products since the 1940s, which parallels the decrease in sperm production and motility in the male population seen today. The speculation is that this phenomenon is caused by growth hormones used in dairy farming with the resultant increase in estrogenic hormonal activity negatively affecting male children. Use milk that is organic, without hormones added, and from cows that are not being overstimulated (in which case, they produce excessive hormones into the milk).

Another example is bisphenol A, a synthetic compound found in plastics and epoxy resins. It is considered an endocrine disrupter because it is weakly estrogenic and may be contributing to breast cancer. It is used in cans and plastic bottles and leaches into the food. Use bottles and cans that say "BPA-free."

You may have heard of polychlorinated biphenyls known as PCBs used as coolants and lubricants that are implicated in causing cancer. Though banned from use for a long time, they resist degradation and have found their way into our food supply. The only advice I can think of here is to remember the food chain and try to eat less off the top of the chain, where all these xenobiotics are concentrated. There are many foods containing these xenobiotics, and I suspect that time will prove out their harmful nature. Therefore, make an effort to educate yourself, read labels, and shop where foods are sold without these additives.

Refined Products

It used to be that white bread was what the public wanted. It would stay fresh for a long time. The grocer was happy because it could stay on the shelf for a long time, and the consumer was happy because it would stay soft at home. It was easier to digest than other coarse breads. We could make it look brown with a little caramel coloring in it just in case we wanted it to look more real. And occasionally they would add back vitamins and call the product "enriched."

But people's nutrition suffered. By removing the perishable "germ" from the bread, we removed valuable vitamins that enabled us to digest it. By removing the bran, the indigestible fiber, we removed that part of nature that helped us regularize our bowel habits, lower cholesterol, and remove toxins, which I consider important in preventing cancer. The solution, as discussed above in the carbohydrate section, is to eat whole (unrefined) grains called "complex carbohydrates" and cook with unrefined flours.

Frozen and Canned Foods

People are often shocked to find out that I do not recommend eating foods that have been frozen or canned. I know it's convenient and often necessary, but consider the following. Oftentimes, these products have salt, sugars, additives, and preservatives; however, my major objection is based upon Ayurvedic (the science of longevity) theory about food energy. I think of it like this. Quite simply, which tastes better, the fresh orange juice or the frozen orange juice? The fresh juice tastes better because its energy is considered more alive than the processed and frozen juice. Remember our discussion earlier about the difference in energy found in flesh foods versus the energy found in beans and peas. Whereas the flesh foods decay under damp conditions, the legumes actually come alive and sprout, demonstrating that they contain a spark of life force within them. Foods that are less processed and are "alive" can give that life energy to you when you consume them.

Breakfast, Lunch, Snack, and Dinner Ideas

Suggestions that Incorporate the Previous Principles

Breakfast

Oatmeal (sugar) or other whole grains as discussed with butter (good fats) or eggs (good fat)
Soaked almonds or other nuts (good fats and protein), apple, or other fruit (sugar), e.g., Brazil nuts and a fig or two
Whole-fat yogurt (fat and protein), fruit (sugar). (I like to slice up an apple or an orange into plain, whole-fat yogurt and occasionally sweeten with maple syrup.)
Whole-grain bread with butter or almond butter

Lunch

Raw salad (sugars, vitamins, and minerals) with avocado (fat) and nuts (protein/fat) or salmon (protein/omega-3 fats) or grass-fed chicken or meats (proteins/fats)
Basmati rice with steamed/roasted vegetables and beans or fish or chicken

Snack

Fruit such as grapes or an apple with a few walnuts/almonds preferably soaked or goji berries or a fig with a few nuts
Raw-food cracker with almond butter or coconut butter or cashew butter

Dinner (Lighter, Especially After the Sun Has Set)

Yogurt and fruit
Salad with a little fish
Whole-grain bread with hummus (chickpea spread)
Soups
Smoothies

Summary—Food for Health and Wellness

Our discussion on sugars educated us on the difference between simple and complex carbohydrates with suggestions about what foods to eat. Use this information and try to avoid the diabetes "epidemic." The discussion on protein followed. There are so many fads and fantasies concerning sugars and proteins. Follow this discussion and eat in a way that supports your life energy and budget, and attempt to avoid cancer and heart disease along with an assorted number of inflammatory conditions. The good fats mentioned next are essentially anti-inflammatory in nature and are valuable in a host of conditions, ranging from high blood pressure, heart disease, and asthma, to acne, elevated triglycerides, learning difficulties, attention deficit hyperactivity disorder, and Alzheimer's prevention. Next, we found out that the beautiful colors in our fruits and vegetables are there to protect us from the likes of prostate cancer, breast cancer, osteoporosis, cataracts, and varicose veins, to name just a few. In the last section of the "good food," we used a few examples and supported the notion that carefully selected vitamins will help specific health conditions (prostate cancer), specific times in a person's life (bone loss in the menopausal and elderly), specific states (protection from cigarette smoke and the effects of alcohol or protecting the healthy cells during chemotherapy treatment for cancer), or general immune support during an emotionally stressful time or during the flu season.

We then discussed what foods to avoid. We considered the harmful effects of xenobiotics and their prevalence in our food supply and touched on the effects of estrogens as a possible correlation with breast cancer in women and possibly interfering with male sexual development. I then briefly discussed polyunsaturated fats and hydrogenated fats. These are harmful fats and best avoided. Lastly, we discussed a simple but eye-opening concept of live versus dead energy in discussing refined, frozen, and canned foods and offered some examples for breakfast, lunch, and dinner.

Choose live foods wherever possible.

9

A Taste of Ayurvedic Food Therapy

THIS SCIENCE HAS a lot to say about which foods will benefit you depending on your Kapha, Pitta, or Vata constitution. Remember, your constitution will usually be a combination of two of the three major elements. The following is a brief review of the Ayurvedic classification of foods. For real case examples of how I have used food as medicine for each specific constitution, see the discussion under Ayurveda in chapter 2.

What follows here is a brief description and classification of some foods and their effects on the three classic constitutional types. For a more extensive listing of foods and their Ayurvedic properties, I refer you to the tables of foods and their Ayurvedic effects in Dr. Vasant Lad's book entitled *AYURVEDA: The Science of Self-Healing*[31] and *Diet and Nutrition* by Rudolph Ballentine, MD.[32]

Kapha Constitutional Type in Review

Please refer to chapter 6 for a more detailed description. In brief review, the properties of the elements making up Kapha are cold, wet, and, stable. As the earth is stable, we think of our bones, muscles, and mucous membranes as representing the stable, solid, structural part of us. Therefore, he or she may look large, muscular to heavy, big-boned, with a tendency to overweight. They are chilly rather than warm and as mentioned earlier, they tend to be slow in action, fertile, jolly, graceful, loving, emotionally stable, and calm, bringing a sense of cohesiveness and security to those around them. They project stability and solidness both physically and emotionally.

Food Therapy

Foods exhibiting the tastes of sweet, sour, or salty or the properties of cold, wet, and heavy will enhance the elements of earth and water, which make up the Kapha constitution of our body/mind. Here are a few examples.

Sweet: sugar, rice, wheat, oatmeal (rather than dry oats), milk, cream, butter, bananas, oranges, melons, sweet grapes and sweet fruits, avocado, coconut, and many nuts such as almonds and cashews
Sour: cheese, yogurt, tomatoes, plums, vinegar, sour fruits such as sour pineapples, sour grapes, strawberries, unripe fruit
Salty: salt, sea vegetables, or any food containing added salt
Flesh foods: beef (note the heavy consistency), fish (note the watery consistency)

Imbalance

All these foods will stimulate the tendency toward Kapha expression. When conditions cause Kapha to become unbalanced and excessive as discussed in chapter 6, Kapha will become an exaggeration of its normal tendencies. Slow becomes inactive. Stability turns to stagnation, lethargy, dullness, and depression, and steadfastness becomes stubbornness and procrastination. In the body, imbalance will exaggerate the earthy elements expressing itself as tumors, fibroid growths, and weight gain. The mucous membranes, representing the watery elements, will become affected and promote asthma, bronchitis, sinusitis, tonsillitis, ear infections, upper-respiratory infections, and arthritis. They are all considered Kapha diseases.

Balance Kapha

1. Decrease Kapha—stop sweet, sour, salty, and fleshy foods as mentioned above
2. Increase Pitta and Vata

Pungent will increase Pitta: spices such as cayenne, chili peppers, garlic, ginger, cumin, onions, radishes, and honey (metabolized as fire)
Astringent will increase Vata: beans, lentils, green apples, green bananas, pears, cabbage, broccoli, cauliflower, potatoes, and turmeric
Bitter will increase Vata: bitter greens such as romaine lettuce, endive, chicory, spinach and leafy greens in general, bitter cucumbers, lemon rind, turmeric, and fennel

Pitta Constitutional Type in Review

Please see chapter 6 for a more detailed description. In brief review, Pitta represents the energy of fire and includes the properties of hot, oily, and irritable. As such, we think of heat, burning flames and light. Pitta is the energy that transforms one thing into another, whether it is food in the digestive tract being changed into energy or an idea in our mind that needs to be formulated and expressed. In the body, this fire is said to express itself via the digestive enzymes, which facilitate digestion as well as affecting the health of the skin, eye, and circulatory system. In the mind, this fire represents "lighting up" of insight, usually represented as a light bulb coming on that gives clarity and understanding to a situation.

Food Therapy

Foods that exhibit the tastes of sour, salty, and pungent will enhance the properties of the element of fire, which make up the Pitta constitution in our body/mind.

Sour: see above
Salty: see above
Pungent: spices such as cayenne, chili peppers, garlic, ginger, cumin, onions, radishes, and honey (metabolized as fire)

Imbalance

To review the basic concepts of balancing Pitta in chapter 6, when conditions cause Pitta to become excessive, the fire behind transformational energy now becomes destructive and begins to "burn" the individual, producing inflammation. The skin becomes red, hot, itchy, burning, and inflamed. Inflammatory conditions such as acid reflux, gastritis, colitis, gallbladder problems, and high blood pressure may result. In the mind, focus and intensity turn to irritability, impatience, and anger, literally burning themselves or others with their words or behaviors.

Balance Pitta

1. Decrease Pitta—stop sour, salty, and pungent foods (as above) and serve food cool
2. Increase Kapha and Vata

Sweet will increase Kapha: sugar, rice, wheat, oatmeal (rather than dry oats), milk, cream, butter, bananas, oranges, melons, sweet grapes, and sweet fruits
Astringent will decrease Pita and increase Vata: beans, lentils, apples, pears, cabbage, broccoli, cauliflower, potatoes, and turmeric
Bitter will increase Vata: bitter greens such as romaine lettuce, endive, chicory, spinach and leafy greens in general, bitter cucumbers, lemon rind, turmeric, and fennel

Vata Constitutional Type in Review

For more detail, please see chapter 6. Briefly, the Vata type exhibits the properties of cold, dry, irregular, active, unstable, empty, and dark. We used the example of wind and space dominating the person's body/mind where movement and flow are the predominant energies. Compared to earth's stability, wind is unstable and irregular, and where fire is hot and light, space is dark and empty. Physically, the person is likely to be chilly rather than hot like Pitta (fire), smaller, thin, or wiry rather than large, muscular, or plump like Kapha (earth). The tendency to dryness may cause the skin to appear rough and dry and wrinkled. Emotionally, when balanced, Vata is energetic, enthusiastic, spirited, and creative.

Food Therapy

Foods that stimulate the tastes of astringent and bitter will enhance the properties of the elements of wind and space, which make up the Vata constitution in the body/mind.

> *Astringent*: beans, lentils, potatoes, green apples, pears, cabbage, broccoli, cauliflower, and turmeric
> *Bitter*: bitter cucumbers, lemon rind, turmeric, fennel, and bitter greens such as romaine lettuce, endive, chicory, spinach, and leafy greens in general

Imbalance

As discussed in chapter 6, when Vata becomes excessive, Vata will become an exaggeration of its normal self. Physically, dry skin becomes cracked. It is taught that natural downward-directed energy (*apana vayu*) becomes blocked and reverses direction and rises in the body. This phenomenon becomes responsible for many gastrointestinal symptoms, such as constipation and gas and bloating after eating. This rising energy may adversely affect the organ systems higher up in the body, such as the heart, causing arrhythmias or the sinuses, causing sinusitis, or the head, causing headache, dizziness, and anxiety.

Sleep becomes a problem, and insomnia is common. The whole makeup appears restless, nervous (windy), and spacey (*akasha*), first here, now there. He or she doesn't have his or her feet on the ground, forgets appointments, and becomes easily distractible as creativity turns to dissipation, and enthusiasm turns to anxiety and fear.

Balance Vata

1. Keep hydrated and serve food and drink warm
2. Decrease Vata—stop astringent and bitter foods
3. Increase Kapha and Pitta

Sweet will increase Kapha: sugar, rice, wheat, oatmeal (rather than dry oats), milk, cream, butter, bananas, oranges, melons, sweet grapes, and sweet fruits
Sour will increase Kapha and Pitta: cheese, yogurt, tomatoes, plums, vinegar, sour fruits such as sour pineapples, and sour grapes
Salty will increase Kapha and Pitta: salt, sea vegetables, or any foods with added salt

10

Herbs and Botanicals Used as Medicine

Herbal/Botanical Medicine

As stated before, plant life has provided us with food and medicine. Botanical medicine is a vast, complex subject and medical art with a long and noble history. Herbal medicines, often called "botanicals," utilize part of a plant (flowers, stems, roots, fruit, or bark) to treat the medical symptoms of a person or animal. It is thought that herbs have been used as spices and medicines for thousands of years. Manuscripts and writings have been recorded from the countries of India and China and later in Greek and Roman writings, including those of Hippocrates, the Greek physician considered by many to be the father of modern medicine.

Many modern drugs in use today have an herbal origin such as foxglove (digitalis), used for various heart conditions, and aspirin (salicylic acid from willow bark), used as an anti-inflammatory. The World Health Organization (WHO) estimates that thirty-five thousand to seventy thousand species of plants are used for medicinal purposes around the world.[33] In developing countries, according to WHO estimates, up to 80 percent of the population depend on them.[34] In India, where traditional Ayurvedic medicine employs over twelve hundred different herbs, herbal medicine is regularly used by about 65 percent of the population.[35]

My intention here is to give you a taste (no pun intended) of how I use herbs in my medical practice because I find them so helpful, easy to use, and cost-effective with fewer side effects, compared to modern pharmaceuticals. Here at the clinic, we use a few of the many herbs available to help people. Earlier, when introducing herbology in the "tools for life" in chapter 4, I mentioned echinacea and turmeric. I will now list a few more of our commonly used herbs and their indications of action with true case histories when appropriate.

Berberis Vulgaris (European Barberry)

This plant grows as a shrub in Europe, Africa, Asia, North America, and elsewhere. I actually use it in a one-tenth dilution prepared in alcohol as a tincture. I prescribe this for people with kidney stones. *Berberis* helps the stones pass through the ducts (ureters) that lead from the kidneys to the bladder by helping the smooth muscles that line the ureters relax so the stone can pass. *Berberis* can save you a trip to the emergency room!

Chelidonium Majus (Greater Celandine)

It is native to Europe and America. I use this herb almost exclusively to promote liver health and to aid in digestion. If I find that a patient has a history of bloating and gas after eating, I will look at his or her tongue. Often, it will show teeth marks, indicating a swollen tongue, and we relate this sign to liver issues. The liver has an important digestive function that is overlooked in modern medicine as a treatment intervention. Our teachers stated, "The liver has no teeth," meaning if we gulp our food rather than chew it, this creates a burden for the liver and may result in digestive problems.

Chelidonium (and dandelion and milk thistle) to the rescue. Their actions are said to be cholagogic and choleretic, which serve to stimulate the flow of bile and dilute the bile, resulting in improved liver functioning and digestion. Dandelion leaves are said to "detox" the liver probably because they act the same way. I often give patients a tincture of dandelion and *Chelidonium* combined in a two-to-one ratio, with instructions to take fifteen drops of the mixture in one teaspoon of water twenty minutes before meals. I've seen it help patients by reducing gas and bloating. Milk thistle (*Silybum marianum*, sometimes called "silymarin") can be used this way also, but I tend to use it to help restore the health of liver cells affected by alcohol, drugs, or modern medicines. The liver is the major organ to detoxify and eliminate these substances and may become damaged from prolonged exposure to them.

Chaste Tree (Vitex Agnus-Castus)

Apparently in ancient times, people in various situations considered this plant to be an aphrodisiac, having the ability to lower the sexual appetite, hence the name "chaste tree." On the other hand, I was taught that this herb helps stimulate follicular growth in the ovaries of women. In order to have sufficient levels of progesterone, ovulation must take place in a follicle. That part of the ovarian tissue that remains after a follicle ruptures is called a "corpus luteum." It is the corpus luteum that produces progesterone. Many women in their thirties and forties are not ovulating as often as they think they are and may even be anovulatory (without ovulation). Therefore, if ovulation does not take place, progesterone is not made in the ovaries.

When working with a woman's health, we suspect that a woman has less progesterone than optimal if she has PMS symptoms such as anxiety, irritability, mood swings, and insomnia or complains of dry eyes, fat gain around the hips and thighs, fatigue, foggy thinking, memory loss, and other symptoms. We often ask her to do a saliva test to measure her hormones. If we document that her progesterone is low and out of balance with estrogen, before giving bioidentical progesterone, we will prescribe chaste tree as a natural alternative to help her ovaries ripen follicles and produce progesterone. Many women who are still having menstrual cycles improve with using chaste tree alone.

Calendula Officinalis (Pot Marigold)

I love *Calendula*!

Calendula has many traditional uses, but I use it exclusively as a wound-healing medicinal herb. I repeat: I love *Calendula*. It's a miracle plant for cuts and open wounds. I call it thus because I have seen it work so magnificently. Firstly, when someone is cut, there is pain and trauma. *Calendula*, as a cream or tincture, can take the trauma right out of the wound almost instantly. People feel better immediately. Secondly, the wounds seem to close up like magic! Within twenty-four hours, there is often complete healing with little to no evidence of the cut ever having been there! Thirdly, it seems to be strongly antibacterial, as I have never used a skin antibiotic for open wounds—just *Calendula*.

Calendula Stories

I have used it for cuts on the skin of my children and have literally watched the open wounds close up with no infection. I prescribe it after dental work that involves cutting. At one point in my life, I had gum surgery, and I was able to swish with a *Calendula*-water mixture as part of a natural approach to healing and pain and was able to avoid pain medication altogether.

Another time, my wife, while taking our infant son out of the car seat, slammed the car door to come in to the house, but her finger was caught in the door, and she could not pull it out. She opened the door, and her finger was gushing with blood and beginning to swell. She ran into the house and made a *Calendula*-water tincture and soaked her finger several times that day. The next day, to her surprise, the swelling was down with the wound looking good and closing up, and no stitches were necessary.

The most dramatic experience I remember with the herb took place at the beginning of my holistic medical training. A colleague was attempting to remove snow from the common walk leading up to the clinic, and he accidently got his fingers caught in the blade of the snowblower. As someone called the paramedics, we wrapped his hand and fingers in gauze dressing soaked with *Calendula* tincture. Later that day, we heard that his fingers were going to be all right, and there was no sign of infection. I love *Calendula* and would never leave home (vacation or other travels) without it.

Licorice (Root of Glycyrrhiza Glabra)

We all think of licorice as the red or black candy we grew up with; however, this plant (actually a legume) has great medicinal value for the digestive tract. When glycyrrhizic acid is removed from licorice (a sweet-tasting compound from licorice root that can potentially cause hypertension), the resulting entity is called "deglycyrrhizinated licorice," or more commonly, DGL.

I have used DGL for patients with acid reflux. It has an ability to coat the stomach and protect it from the ravages of stomach acid. Recently, I treated a forty-eight-year-old woman who was very stressed about an upcoming job change. She presented with a diagnosis of a peptic stomach ulcer and stated that she had a tendency to develop ulcers when stressed. She was going to see her gastroenterologist in a couple of weeks for a biopsy, and she asked if there was anything natural she could do. I suggested she try DGL and drink one glass of cabbage juice per day.

She said, "I'll skip the juice, but I'll try the DGL."

Three weeks later, she came to the office for a return visit and announced she had visited her gastrointestinal physician who performed an endoscopy (tube through the mouth into the stomach). He told her, "There is no sign of an ulcer. It's completely healed. I can't biopsy it because everything is normal! Whatever you're doing, keep it up."

If you're having problems with acid reflux or peptic ulcers, try to get to the root of the problem with dietary correction or stress reduction. In the meantime, you can treat it naturally with DGL under the guidance of a professional.

These are a few of the foods and plants that I have used as herbs to treat patients. At this point, I would like to move to the next category of physical health and say a few words about exercise.

11

Exercise

Golden Rules of Exercise

HERE ARE SOME "golden rules" of exercise that I have learned over the years. I trust them to keep me safe, consider them very important, and suggest these to my patients and use them personally. The bottom line is to exercise mindfully.

Awareness. Stay conscious of your body and your surroundings. Use the five senses to root yourself in the moment during your activity.

Nonharming. Stay within your capacity. If you do more than you should, you may hurt yourself. Respect yourself this way. Embrace the idea that you do have an optimal range for activity with human limitations, and it's a nurturing thing to do when you stay in that safe zone without overdoing or underdoing. Any less or any more is not right.

One Activity. Do not do two things at once. Do not read while walking and ideally stop talking or listening to music and concentrate on what you're doing in the moment. That way, the activity becomes an exercise in concentration and helps you form what the yogis call a "one-pointed mind," i.e., building up your capacity to focus mindfully on anything! Also, you're less likely to do anything to hurt yourself like overexert a muscle or hyperextend a joint while you're "in concentration" because you're tuned in to your body's feedback, and you are "right there" when your body tells you to slow down or back off or says "enough."
Breathe. Use your breath as you move. As you walk, you can coordinate your inhalation and exhalation with your stride. For example, you can walk four paces with inhalation and four with exhalation. Your breath will protect you.

Types of Exercise

1. Flexibility

Goals: avoid arthritis, loss of mobility, pain in the joints, and be able to pick something up off the floor without injury

Yoga

An old yogic saying states, "You're as young as your spine." There are no blood vessels in the joints of the body, so it is taught that the way we keep them healthy is to move them.

I believe that gentle yoga postures, when practiced using the mindfulness principles previously talked about, promote a safe way of keeping the joints mobile and the muscles, tendons, and ligaments flexible.

Tai Chi

These gentle, flowing movements done in coordination with the breath become a moving meditation. Tai chi consists of slow, intentional arm and leg movements accompanied with breathing that is synchronized with each movement, resulting in a wonderful sense of centeredness within one's body and balance on one's feet. The movements promote flexibility, strength, balance, and coordination and are an excellent exercise to incorporate as one ages to maintain a sense of "springy youthfulness."

Feldenkrais® Therapy

I had the pleasure of meeting Moshe Feldenkrais. He taught a method of gentle directed body movements that ended up creating a more mobile body. (Please see chapter 4 for a fuller discussion.)

2. Balance

Goals: avoid falling and enjoy a sense of physical stability

Yoga

There are many postures that promote balance such as the standing postures, including the forward bend, the side bend, and the tree posture where you learn to stand on one leg with your arms in various positions (simulating a tree), and the shoulder stand where you are balancing upside down. (figure 5-2)

Tai Chi

This can be done as mentioned above.

Walking and Breathing

As mentioned above, try coordinating the breath with walking. One way to do this is to inhale two or three strides and then exhale two or three strides. Another way is to visualize the following: as you walk, inhale upward through the bottoms of your feet up through your legs to your waist and then visualize the exhalation back downward through your legs into your feet and into the ground. I use this exercise for patients who appear unsteady on their feet and who need grounding.

3. Strength and Endurance

Goals: confidence to lift burdens without injury and go the distance physically when needed

Weight-Bearing Exercise

I enjoy using free weights and elastic bands to put resistance against the muscles and make them "work." These activities promote strength and help keep bones strong. The best way to absorb calcium from your food into your bones and to create strong bones is to stimulate them using weight-bearing exercise. Use a qualified trainer to show you how to do it properly so you won't hurt yourself.

Yoga

There are many yoga postures that build strength, usually in combination with balance such as the headstand, cradle, and others.

Walking

As you walk, the pressure exerted on the spine helps build strong bone. Some people add small weights in their hands. Others choose to walk up a hill or an incline.

4. Aerobic Fitness

Goals: cardiac fitness and longevity

Everyone knows that moving your body and getting your heart rate up in a safe way can improve your heart health and lower blood pressure; improve your immune system; lower rates of obesity while converting fat to muscle; reduce diabetes, cancer, and osteoporosis; improve memory and brain function; and help you live longer and have an increased sense of well-being. But what you didn't know is how little activity you actually need to pull this off!

Classically, subtract your age from 220, and 60 to 70 percent of the result should be your pulse rate. For example, if you're 45, then 45 subtracted from 220 equals 175, and 60 percent of that is 105. Theoretically, you can exercise for a while with your heart rate up to 105, and that's considered a safe form of aerobic exercise.

Exercise, Fitness, and Longevity

Good news. Take a look at a part of this study that explored the effect of exercise and fitness on the risk of all-cause mortality in men and women.[36] (See figure 11-1.)

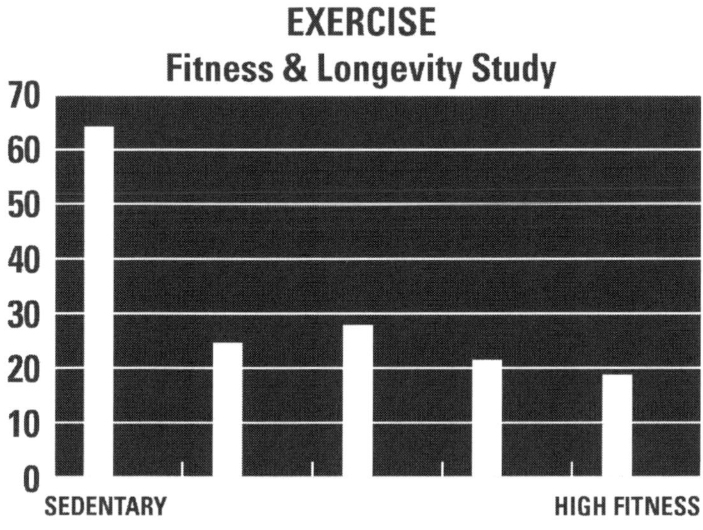

Figure 11-1.

At first glance, with death rates on the left side of the graph and exercise on the bottom, it shows the more exercise one did, the lower the mortality rate. You think to yourself, "of course, everybody knows that exercise will help you live longer." But look closer.

(See figure 11-2.)

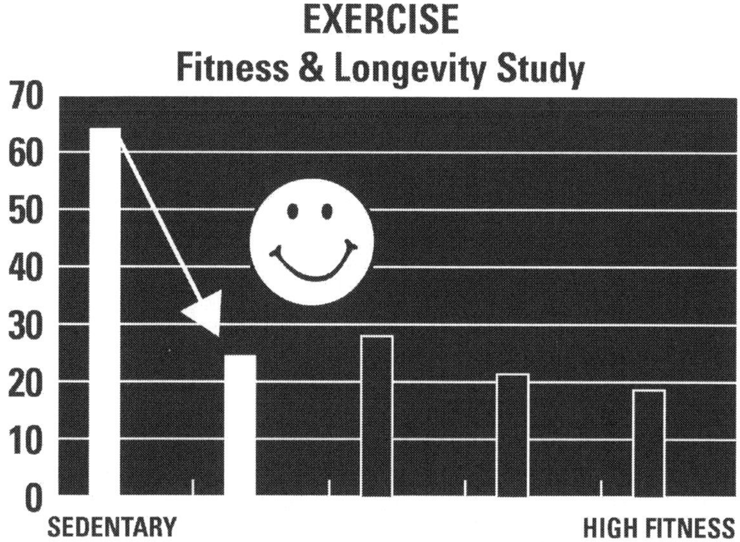

Figure 11-2.

Just stop being sedentary!

Philip J. Hilts mentioned this study in his *New York Times* article entitled "Exercise and Longevity: A Little Goes a Long Way." [8] He wrote, "The most striking finding was that the biggest health gain came from just getting out of the most sedentary category, rather than seeking the fitness achieved by dedicated athletes."

This is remarkable, and my patients really sit up and take notice of this. Look at the graph and see why the emoji is smiling. To get the benefit of longevity, all you have to do is accomplish enough exercise to fit into the graph one bar over from sedentary! Stop being sedentary! I have to repeat this to them. My interpretation is that if you stop sitting and *do something*, i.e., *almost anything*, then your chances of dying drop near the level of someone at high fitness who works out long and hard, shown by the bar all the way over to the right of the graph.

So what is "something, almost anything"? Some use the term "moderate intensity," but I believe it is walking! Gentle biking! Slow swimming! Patients are shocked that they can actually walk and dramatically drop their risk of mortality, as the study appears to be independent of family history, diet, or stress and only mentions testing the variable of exercise. Now notice the next illustration and take heed. (See figure 11-3.)

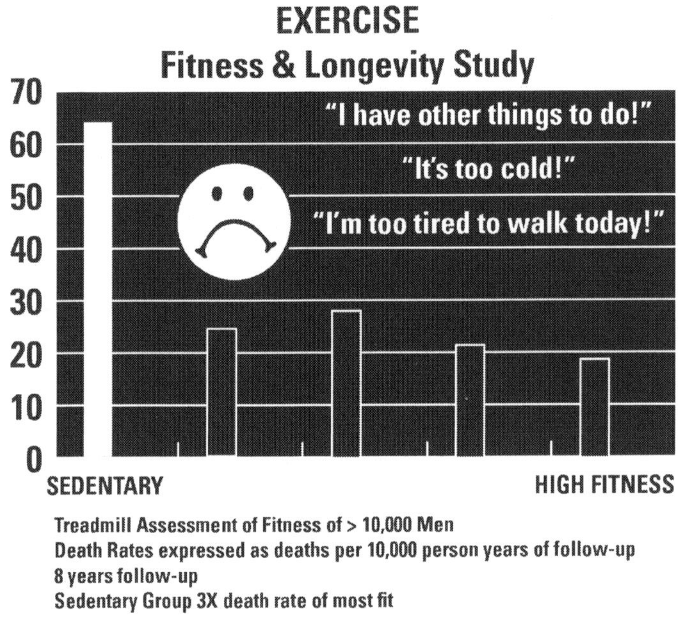

Figure 11-3.

Excuses, excuses, excuses.

A sedentary lifestyle equals a higher rate of all-cause death.

I have a collection of reasons that people do not exercise, including the three in figure 11-3. Do you see yourself in the following list?

- "I itch."
- "It's too cold."
- "I'm too tired to walk today."
- "I have to take my son to school three times a week."
- "Winter is a problem."
- "I have to get ready for a garage sale."
- "There is always something to do."
- "I don't have time."
- "I procrastinate."
- "I'm lazy."
- "I have no reason."
- "I have not made the time."
- "I don't try."
- "I don't have the opportunity."
- "I hurt."
- "I have prior priorities."
- "I don't like to."
- "I'm sporadic."
- "It's not exciting."
- "I have a crazy lifestyle."
- "I have a crazy work schedule."
- "I don't have an excuse."

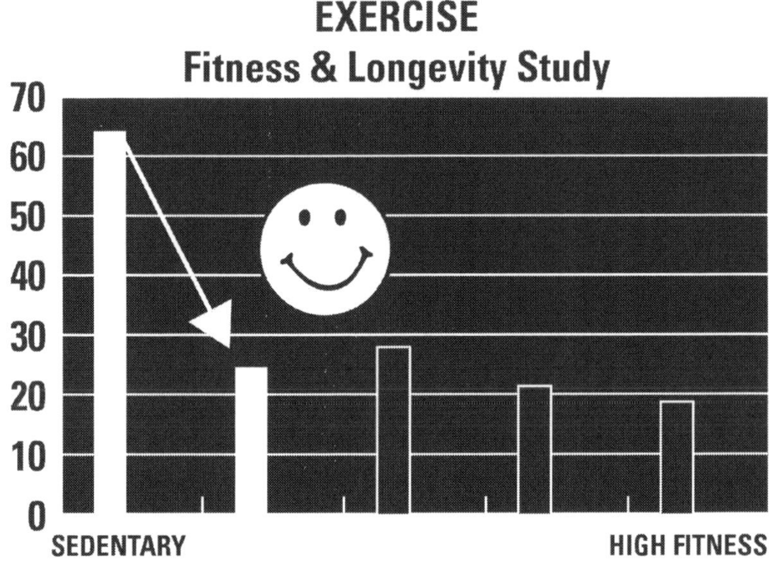

Figure 11-4.

Once again, I want to restate the happy findings from this study because I really want you to sit up and take notice that just a little exercise will help you live longer. (See figure 11-4.)

Exercise and Breast-Cancer Prevention

Here is a study that documents the value of exercise as a cancer-prevention strategy for women.[38]

EXERCISE

Regular moderate, physical exercise strengthens the heart, reduces body fat, and boosts the immune system. But did you know that exercise also reduces the risk of breast cancer by almost 40%? A study published in the May 1, 1997 issue of the *New England Journal of Medicine* followed 25,624 women over 13 years. **They found a 37% risk reduction in women who engaged in moderate exercise for at least four hours a week.**

As you can see, there are many benefits to exercise if done in a moderate and sensible way. I recommend it for flexibility, balance, strength/endurance, and aerobic fitness. Some positive side effects include bone health, brain health, immune support, cancer prevention, and emotional stability.

Enjoy Your Own Program

I try to design my week to contain these four forms of exercise. For example, I wake up and do some gentle joints and glands exercise (flexibility) followed by twenty minutes of walking or gentle aerobic exercise. I encourage a light weights program two to three times a week initiated with the instruction of a trainer (strength and endurance). I like to practice my tai chi once a week. Be creative. Many people will use tai chi or another form of martial art that combines all four of the above suggestions. My wife likes to hike up and down the hill nearby. This involves aerobic fitness, strength, endurance, balance, and willpower. Gardening involves bending, lifting, and balance. How about walking around your block for twenty minutes or gentle biking, swimming, or putting on some music and dancing? The important thing is to make a habit of exercise. How do you do that? It's much easier to do if you have fun with it. Remember to use moderation and personalize it—make it fit you. Perhaps Ayurveda can give us a few tips about choosing an exercise program that fits your body/mind type.

Exercise for Your Ayurvedic Body Type

Please refer back to chapter 6 to identify your Ayurvedic constitution.

Exercise for Kapha (Earthy, Solid, Stolid, Substantial)

Ayurveda suggests that, being stable as you are, to spice it up (Pitta) and jazz it up (Vata).

Exchange jogging for jazzercise, avoid the same old, same old routine by varying weight machines or using free weights and bands, or add impromptu sessions that spice up the routine.

If you walk, add bursts of sprints or skipping (easy on the knees). If biking, change the pace, change the company, or change the route! If swimming, change the stroke, and change up indoors and outdoors water. Remember, the warmer and more creative, the better.

These exercise suggestions will help "lighten up" the heavy, solid, stolid part of your body/mind and bring out your creativity.

Exercise for Pitta Type (Hot, Fiery, Intense, Irritable)

Try exercising in such a way as to minimize intensity and burnout. Try team sports rather than individual competition and emphasize enjoyment and cooperation rather than winning versus losing or domination versus submission. This would balance the intensity and competitive fire. For example, switch from singles tennis to doubles or from handball to team sports like volleyball or basketball. Avoid overheating during exercise; cooler is better. Exercise in nature, surrounded by natural beauty.

All these strategies help balance Pitta, which will promote relaxation, calmness, and patience, while still allowing you to be focused and to get the job done.

Exercise for Vata (Cold, Dry, Irregular, Active, Unstable)

Think of yourself as the wind. What exercises balance wind? Unlike earthy Kapha, you will benefit from a steady, regularly scheduled routine as you exchange creativity for stability. Same day, same hour, same activity—all the better. You may consider this boring, but soon you will realize an internal stability that benefits you (and allows you to express your creativity in a grounded, functional way). Exercising by running or walking with your feet contacting the earth will quite literally ground you. Add synchronized breathing with the movements (tai chi or walking and breathing), and you will feel centered in a way that spells bliss for a windy, ephemeral personality. Swimming in lukewarm water (not cold) complements the dry and chilly tendency. Where Pitta avoids sun, you with your tendency to chilliness love exercising in the warmth, and the hotter the better.

If you have a Vata tendency and you use these tips, exercise will help create warmth, routine, and stability both physically and emotionally.

Exercise and Health

As you can see, there are many benefits to exercise if done in a moderate and sensible way. I recommend it for flexibility, balance, strength, endurance, and aerobic fitness. Some positive side effects include bone health, brain health, immune support, cancer prevention, and emotional stability.

Energy—the Bridge between the Mind and the Body

Using terminology from *Sankhya* philosophy as discussed in chapter 3, the health of the *annamaya kosha*, i.e., the physical sheath, is affected by food and exercise. Now let's turn to the *pranamaya kosha*, or energy sheath, and try to define it as well as find out how to affect it for greater health and wellness. I think of this discussion as progressing along a path of consciousness from obvious to subtle, from outward to inward, and from superficial to the next layer of depth of our humanness.

12

Energy Medicine—My Experiences

Introduction

Many traditions describe a nonphysical, energetic life force or vital energy that courses through our bodies and minds to help sustain our health. What follows are some of my experiences with this vast and complex, almost magical field of energy healing.

Yoga and Breathing

The yogic tradition states that there is a vital life force that sustains our body/mind. This force or energy is called "*prana*" and functions in the body/mind by flowing through a vast and complex system of subtle-energy channels called "*nadis*." There are seventy-two thousand *nadis*. The previously described chakras represent major intersections of *nadis*, rather like a turning circle represents the intersection of several feeder streets feeding into the circle. Proper food, posture, exercise, and thinking can help facilitate the flow of *prana*. According to tradition, the breath is a subtle form of *prana*, and by consciously breathing, we can use the breath to regulate the flow of *prana*. This is done through a series of techniques working with the breath in several ways. These techniques and the idea of breath regulation are referred to as *pranayama*, the science of breath control or regulation.

The metaphor I was taught to think of was the following: You have a kite, and you're regulating its flight by guiding the string. You can control the string directly, which indirectly controls the kite. Now by applying this metaphor, think of using the breath (similar to the string) to direct the energy to achieve desired results; i.e., just as the string controls the kite, the breath controls the *prana* and regulates your energy for specific goals.

Here are some common breathing techniques we work with on an everyday basis as examples of using energy to help ourselves achieve our goals. Note that even though we use our physical body, the end result is to establish a certain kind of energy.

Calming Breath—Gentle Diaphragmatic (Belly) Breathing

For Children

When my children were little, I taught them abdominal breathing to help them fall asleep by placing my hand on their tummies and gently counting the breaths. With every inhalation, their bellies would rise, and with each exhalation, their bellies would fall. Each time their bellies rose and fell, I counted one breath. Usually, they never made it past a count of thirty and were sound asleep.

For Adults

Similar to above, begin by placing the hand on the abdomen with the bottom of the hand at the level of the belly button, and gently count the breaths using the following guidelines.

Have the breath be continuous without any pauses or jerkiness. Have inhalation go continuously into exhalation, and exhalation goes right into inhalation. This produces a wonderful calm.

Have inhalation equal exhalation in time and be equal in length in terms of abdominal expansion.

Have the breath be quiet without noise.

Breathe through the nose if possible.

Energizing Breath (*Bhastrika*)

This breath exercise is designed to invigorate and revitalize one's energy by moving the *prana* around the pathways in a vigorous way. It's done by actively contracting the abdomen and bringing the belly button back toward the spine (exhalation) and then actively expanding the abdomen with the belly button coming back out in a protruded manner. This is done moderately fast and is best learned under supervision of a teacher.

Cleansing Breath (*Kapalbhati*)

This breath is designed to cleanse toxins through the lungs. The motion of the abdomen is the same as *bhastrika*, but here we have an active, crisp exhalation with a passive inhalation. It is commonly taught as follows:

Active exhale for one count, and then allow passive inhalation for four counts.

Again, one should learn from a qualified instructor.

Premeditative Breath

This breathing technique can be used to reduce anxiety or prepare one for meditation. A simple method involves focusing the mind at the spot where the upper lip and nose intersect. Become aware of the breath as it exits and enters both nostrils at the same time. Sense how the air feels cooler coming in and warmer going out. One may choose to exhale and inhale through one nostril, then switch over and exhale and inhale through the other nostril. Using this method, the student focuses on the air as it comes through each nostril. This may be repeated a few times and is called alternate-nostril breathing. There are a few variations to this breathing technique, and it's best to consult a qualified teacher to help you learn it properly.

Ordinarily, during the day and depending upon one's activity, the left nostril is active (easier to breathe through), and the right nostril is passive or vice versa. However, after several rounds of exhalation and inhalation during alternate-nostril breathing or simply focusing on the spot between the nostrils as described above, the flow of the breath in both nostrils becomes balanced. This is said to balance the parasympathetic and sympathetic sides of the autonomic nervous system and results in a calm, alert, and uplifting consciousness with a focused mind. Now we can direct the mind toward prayer, contemplation, or meditation. More about this subject can be found in chapter 19.

Traditional Chinese Medicine

In traditional Chinese medicine, the concept theorizes energy (*chi*) flowing through pathways called *meridians*. Disease may be a result of inhibited flow or too much flow of energy through these pathways. Herbal preparations, touch (acupressure), or fine needles (acupuncture) are applied to points in the meridians where energy might be deficient or excessive to help the energy flow through the meridians in a balanced way and thus deliver the right amount of energy to the organs they are responsible for. Tai chi is an exercise consisting of flowing body movements designed to move the *chi* throughout the meridians and thus sustain health.

Aikido

In Japan, the energy concept is called "Qi." The martial art called "aikido" elevates the concept of energy in its movements. Aikido means "*Ai*" (unifying) "*ki*" (spirit or energy) "*do*" (path). The concept is translated as the way of harmony with spirit/energy/path.

I had already taken tai chi for many years and would always try to feel the energy in the movements of my arms, legs, and torso. My first "ah-ha" experience of the concept of energy came to me when I was taught the "unbendable arm" in an aikido class.

Imagine that someone is standing opposite you with his or her arm held straight out from the horizontal. You try to bend the arm at the elbow, but you can't do it! Even if you're bigger and stronger than the person, you can't do it because his or her energy is flowing through the arm, and it feels like a steel rod is in there! How is this possible?

In this case, the person is directing his or her energy and breath with the mind without using any muscular effort. That person has learned to "extend" the energy by concentrating and focusing the mind on having his or her breath or consciousness flow through the arm in an uninterrupted way. When I would lecture on homeopathy and discuss the concept of energy, I would demonstrate the existence of "energy" by inviting one big guy or two people at the same time to come up from the audience and try to bend my arm. In all the years, no one ever bent my arm (but I did think one or two people would snap it off!).

Herbs

People generally think of plant material as a variation of food, i.e., as a physical substance. Earlier, in the nutrition section, we discussed that foods can have different "energies." Ayurveda states that a glass of frozen orange juice, while having the same vitamins as a glass of fresh juice, is a food of lower energy and is "dead" or stale, called "*tamasic*," and indeed, it tastes different. As mentioned earlier, foods that are overcooked, stale, and loaded with chemicals fall into this category of *tamasic* food. Many herbalists suggest that herbs, just like foods, have an energetic effect on the body/mind. For a more in-depth discussion about the herbs we use, see chapter 10.

13

Homeopathy

Introduction

HOMEOPATHY IS AN energy medicine that has gained a lot of popularity. It is a system of medical therapeutics developed by a German physician, Dr. Samuel Hahnemann (1755–1843). The medicines, or remedies, are prepared from natural substances such as plants, minerals, and animal tissues and are prepared and recognized in accordance with the US Food and Drug Administration. They are nontoxic, used in extremely low doses, and safely used with infants, children, and adults.

Homeopathy is practiced all over the world. In Britain, homeopathy is widely practiced, recognized, and paid for by health insurance plans, as 37 percent of British and 42 percent of family physicians have referred patients to a homeopath. In France, 40 percent of the French public have used homeopathic medicines, and 40 percent of French physicians have prescribed them.[39]

In many European countries, homeopathy is reimbursable under their national health services, and in India there are government-sponsored homeopathic hospitals, clinics, and medical colleges as well as licensed pharmacies. In Latin America, as well as the United States, it is becoming increasingly popular as remedies are increasingly found on shelves in the drugstores and alternative-food stores, and homeopathic practitioners are found in the alternative-therapy sections of medical centers throughout the United States.

How Does It Work?

1. Dilution

Plants, minerals, or animal tissues are made into remedies through a process of diluting and shaking. For example, a piece of red onion (Latin name, *Allium cepa*) may be diluted with distilled water and alcohol by taking one part of an onion and ninety-nine parts of alcohol and water, giving us a 1/100th dilution, commonly referred to, using the roman numeral for one hundred, as a 1C potency. Many dilutions or potencies are used, depending upon whether the practitioner desires a weaker or stronger effect. For example, it is common to put *Allium* through this dilution process thirty times, which results in a remedy referred to as a 30C potency (allium diluted 1/100 × 30). According to the mathematical axiom of Avogadro's number, there cannot be any molecules of onion left in the preparation. Yet this is a very effective and commonly used potency in clinical practice. How is this possible? It cannot be the "herbal" effect of the onion because of the extreme dilution. Instead, think of it this way: the remedy now has the "energy" of the onion without actually having any molecules of onion remaining in the dose. That's why homeopathy is called an "energy medicine."

2. Energy, Not Molecules of Matter

Now when a remedy is given successfully, it is postulated that the energy of the remedy is positively affecting the energy inside the person. This energy inside the person is referred to as his or her "vital force" in homeopathic literature. I personally conceptualize it as the energy of the remedy influencing the *prana* flowing through our *nadis* or meridians inside us, as mentioned earlier, restoring and balancing energy to create health.

3. Law of Similars

When cutting an onion, a healthy person will experience a burning flow of tears in the eyes. When the onion is diluted into a remedy, *Allium cepa*, it is then prescribed for a sick person exhibiting those same (similar) symptoms as part of his or her illness. For example, he or she may be suffering from allergy, hay fever, colds, or flu, characterized by a burning, watery discharge from the eyes (same as onion), and if the person is given the remedy *Allium cepa*, those symptoms clear up! Just as the substance, the onion, can cause symptoms in a healthy person (burning, tears, etc.), it can then stimulate self-healing in a sick person with the same symptoms (allergy or flu symptoms, characterized by burning tears). Homeopathy means "similar-suffering" and is based on this healing law of life called the "law of similars."

Another example would be the herb chamomile. When diluted into the homeopathic remedy Chamomilla and given to a healthy person, the person develops symptoms of irritability and impatience. This is called a homeopathic "proving" and is conducted to find out the potential properties of a substance. In this case, an important aspect of the plant chamomile is shown to produce irritability in a healthy person. Therefore, when the remedy Chamomilla is used according to the "law of similars" and is given to a child with an ear infection and irritability or to a teething baby with swollen gums showing a restless, whiney, snappish irritability, self-healing is stimulated based upon the "law of similars." The child becomes cured, i.e., the ear infection heals up, and the gum inflammation and swelling disappear along with the irritable mood!

What Does Homeopathy Treat?

Homeopathy can be applied to all manner of physical and mental/emotional health issues, from conception through birth, childhood, adulthood, and the challenges of the elderly.

Pregnant Mothers

- Nausea of pregnancy, aches and pains associated with carrying the baby, dysfunctional labor, and postpartum emotional issues; helps to tonify uterine tissue to make delivery easier
- Nursing mothers, e.g., breast infections

Children

- Children respond very well to remedies, and their conditions often clear up rapidly when the right remedy is found. Some commonly treated conditions for children are acute or chronic ear infections, unwanted side effects from vaccinations, eczema, allergies, asthma, ADD, and/or emotional problems. It also helps in the promotion of healthy teething.

Women's Health

- There are many problems specific to women that respond well to homeopathic treatment such as cystitis, yeast difficulties, fibroids, PMS, infertility, perimenopausal, menopausal symptoms, and osteoporosis, to name a few.

Men's Health

- Prostate difficulties, infertility

Adults

- There are too many conditions to list here, and they all respond to treatment. A few of the common conditions that people present with are fatigue, colds and flu, sinusitis, irritable bowel, skin problems, headaches, hypertension, heart problems, arthritis, insect bites, injuries, recovery from accidents or surgeries, anxiety, depression, grief, and transitions in life.

Elderly

- Homeopathy is a gentle and effective way of treating the elderly without creating more problems from the side effects of traditional medications.
- Some issues treated are weakness, joint pain, age-related memory loss, problems with movement, digestion, circulation, and emotional issues related to losses and changes both past and present.

What Does the Doctor Do?

1. Study the Symptoms

The doctor will ask for all your physical and emotional symptoms and try to individualize them, determining what makes these symptoms unique to you, and then he or she will select a remedy based on this information. For example, a thirty-five-year-old woman came to the office complaining of a sore throat and cough (physical history). She also reported she was stressed by carpooling her children and handling their other school needs and had been feeling anxious lately (emotional history).

The doctor further studied the symptoms to find out how they were unique to her. The sore throat was right-sided, felt burning, and was better from hot drinks. Her anxiety was worse from the disorder in her life (others thrive on disorder). These symptoms are now individualized and point to a specific remedy that fits her unique condition (Arsenicum). She was given one dose of Arsenicum, consisting of five pellets melted under the tongue. Within the next twenty-four hours, her sore throat *and* anxiety disappeared.

2. Study the Person

This is a second way of arriving at a prescription. People can be said to have different constitutional types. For example, two men desire help for their headaches, but instead of studying the symptoms of the headache and individualizing their headache symptoms, we will study their constitutional traits and look for a remedy that fits their specific type.

Mr. A. has the following characteristics that are unique to him: he is warm (kicks the covers off at night), is messy (but knows where everything is), is forgetful and spacey (misplaced the keys), collects things (may be a pack rat), is handy, likes to talk (argues, makes speeches, etc.), and often has red itchy rashes on his skin.

Mr. B. has a different constitution. He is serious; holds on to old hurts; is idealistic; feels worse after being consoled; craves salty foods; and suffers with hangnails, cracked lips, and eye problems.

Mr. A. received a dose of the remedy Sulphur, and not only did his headache go away, but he cleaned his house, threw away old "stuff," and found his memory improved. Mr. B. received Natrum Muriaticum (sodium chloride) as a remedy. His headache improved, his disposition became lighter, and he stopped craving chips (salt).

This example demonstrates that by studying the person, we look for his or her individuality and give the remedy that fits his or her constitution, and then self-healing takes place. Homeopathy provides a remedy to fit your unique constitution.

3. Study the Remedy

After studying the symptoms and/or studying the person's constitution, the doctor is now ready to choose a remedy that best fits the history taken. We do this by looking up these symptoms or constitutional characteristics in books or computer programs loaded with information about remedies. For example, many homeopathic books tell us that a right-sided sore throat made better by hot drinks has the remedy Arsenicum as mentioned above. But a left-sided sore throat made worse by hot drinks has Lachesis (made from snake venom). There are hundreds of remedies to choose from, and each remedy has several pages of information about how it affects the entire body and mind of the person. Through a combination of taking a good history to clarify all the patient's important symptoms and then researching and using our experience of our knowledge of the remedies to find the remedy that matches those symptoms, we select a remedy for the person.

4. Follow the Progress

An important question to ask is, "Am I going in the right direction with my health care?" This may sound silly, but this is not discussed much in standard medicine. It usually goes without saying that if the patient's symptoms are better, then the patient is better, and the medical treatment is considered a success. We find this too simplistic and may even be harmful. Therefore, I use the following approaches when evaluating a patient's progress.

An Orderly Relief from the Physical Symptoms

It is stated in the homeopathic literature and I have found in my experience as a physician that deeper and long-lasting healing often comes about when the body takes a path of healing that exhibits the following order: symptoms appearing and then healing from deep to superficial, i.e., from deep within the body to a more superficial part of the body, or from a more important organ to a less important organ, or in the reverse order of the symptoms appearing.

Case Example

A forty-two-year-old woman presented with shortness of breath diagnosed as asthma. She remembered that the onset of her asthma began after using skin creams to treat a rash that was diagnosed as eczema in her childhood. Her childhood eczema had made her very uncomfortable both physically and emotionally. During her homeopathic treatment, we first witnessed her asthma improve, which was, much to her horror, followed by a reappearance of her dreaded eczema condition! After assuring her that her case was going in the right direction, we did not use any creams and waited. Slowly, her eczema disappeared, and she felt fine.

These medical events followed the principles of the correct direction of cure in that we saw the more important and deeper organ (lungs) improve first, followed by the appearance and then healing of the less important and more superficial organ (skin). We also saw the symptoms appear and heal in the reverse order of their coming, i.e., the asthma was the more recent illness and was healed first, followed by the eczema, which was the older condition, and it appeared and was healed last.

Using my experience, I have added the additional following guidelines toward assessing the direction of cure, which reflect a more complete body/mind/life approach.

- Improvement in energy and a sense of well-being
- Mental and emotional clarity
- A restored sense of purpose or meaning in life

Case Example

A twenty-eight-year-old woman complained of PMS symptoms: swollen ankles, stomach upset, insomnia, fatigue, and irritability. After studying the symptoms, the person, and the remedies, we selected Nux Vomica and gave her five pellets under the tongue once each night for a week. An ideal response would be to see healing on all levels such as decreased ankle swelling, increased energy, and a feeling of calm alertness.

Beware of treatments that bring relief of physical symptoms while the person becomes worse on the energy level ("I just don't feel right") and/or worse on a mental level (depressed, confused) or on the spiritual level (deteriorating personal relationships, work and other life choices, or lose his or her sense of rightness).

Case Example

A seventy-two-year-old woman complained of joint pain. A history showed that the pain was better from motion and warmth and worse from rest. She was also unsure about where to live and some important decisions to make. Anti-inflammatory medication had helped with the pain but left her feeling tired. She was beginning to feel discouraged (physical symptoms better, energy and mind worse). A remedy immediately came to mind that usually helps the pain in the joints that is worse from rest and better from motion and warmth. But would it help or hurt her ability to feel, think, and make decisions?

With the whole person in mind, we selected a different remedy that helps with arthritis and discouragement. After one dose of a middle potency, she returned and stated, "I feel my life is in order. I'm beginning to think through things properly and making progress on my living situation, and thank you, my hips and knees are slowly but surely improving."

Side Effects

In my experience, there are few side effects with remedies, due to the fact that they are diluted as they are prepared so that only the "energy" of the substance is given to the person. If an incorrect remedy is given over and over to a person, it is possible for that person to develop symptoms, so be sure to follow the advice of a practitioner who is well trained and experienced in homeopathic medical practice.

In Summary

Homeopathy is a system of medical therapeutics using natural substances in very small doses. It is known and practiced throughout the world. It is becoming increasingly popular in the United States and the world as articles appear in national magazines, new research studies are funded, new training programs and societies emerge, and hospitals embrace holistic medicine programs.

Why the renewed interest? As a practicing physician, I find the ideal medicine would be safe, cost-effective, and useful in the incredible variety of situations as described above. It would work on all levels (physical, energetic, and mental) needed in the daily practice of general medicine. The medicine would be flexible enough to span the age gap from infancy to elderly, and the power should be adjustable so that a weaker or stronger potency can be individualized. Homeopathy fits this picture and gives me a powerful tool in treating the whole person.

14

Flower-Essence Therapy

Introduction

IN THE WORLD of energy medicine, I experience the use of flowers in medicine like gentle poetry. Back in the 1930s, a homeopathic physician from England, Dr. Edward Bach, found his niche by developing a way to use our extensive flower life for physical and emotional health. According to the *Flower Essence Repertory* by Patricia Kaminski and Richard Katz, the essences are prepared from a "sun infusion of flowers in water further diluted and potentized and then preserved with brandy."[40] We use glycerin for those who cannot use medicines in an alcohol base. The medicine is dispensed in a one- or two-ounce dropper bottle, and we recommend six drops four times a day on the tongue or in a teaspoon of water. Similar to homeopathic remedies, the end result is a dilute yet energized representation of the essence of the healing quality of the flower.

Examples

Unresolved Grief

Star of Bethlehem is a deeply restorative remedy used for shock or trauma, either recent or past. Tanya, thirty-two, a young professional woman, was a homeopathic physician who had graduated from medical school in India. During our work together, she confided in me that she felt sad over the loss of her father and had not grieved properly. She said, "I just can't cry." We suggested she begin Star of Bethlehem. She took a few drops of the essence and right there and then began to softly cry and shared how much she missed her father.

Anxiety

Paul, a twenty-eight-year-old teacher, felt anxious about life and confused about his future. He was worried about his parents' health, felt unsatisfied with his career, and felt he was "holding back" in life and not "trusting the universe" anymore. I prescribed a combination of three essences for him: (1) Wild oat (*Bromus ramosus*), indicated for transforming "confusion and indecision about life direction" into finding work that expresses your true life purpose, (2) Mimulus (*Mimulus guttatus*), used for fears about our everyday life events and finding the courage to work with them and grow from them, and (3) Walnut (*Jugulans regia*) for those transitions in life where we need to shift into a new paradigm and really let go of the past, rather than making a small evolutionary next step kind of thing.

Paul took six drops four times a day for one week, and then I saw him in the office.

"I feel better," he said. "I have less anxiety and more direction."

"What do you mean?" I said.

"Well, since I saw you, I put an offer on three townhouses, and the first one fell through. I rejected the second, and I'm waiting on the third. I no longer feel stagnated, and new ideas are flowing. The ideas that pop into my head are more refined."

I'm always amazed when I see change like that—in this case, from the energy of three flowers!

Irritability

Juanita was a seventy-two-year-old happily married Latin-American woman. Her husband was seventy-nine and beginning to suffer from memory loss and a general loss of functioning in other areas of life. As she watched her beloved husband's slow decline, she could not help the feelings of frustration and anger she felt as she picked up the responsibility for two people.

Noting the transition she felt was going on and the persistent feeling of frustration (which incidentally contributed to her high blood pressure), I prescribed (1) Walnut (described above) for the loss of the "old life" as she knew it and to help her transition into a new way of living with him, and (2) Impatiens (*Impatiens glandulifera* pink/mauve). Just like the name indicates, this flower essence helps soothe and cool down the fire of anger, tension, and frustration, to take the edge off and let the mind operate under a more neutral state.

I saw Juanita three weeks later, and she appeared more relaxed.

She stated, "My light-headedness is better, and I think the meds you gave me are helping."

"Why?" I asked.

She responded, "I feel less impatient and more compassionate for his functioning. We argue less. Incidentally, I was also able to talk on the phone with my daughter and felt good about it. My daughter is divorced, drinks alcohol, and is unhappy, and I always argue with her and feel bad after I get off the phone. This time it was different."

Trauma and Other Uses

Flower essences can be used for a whole host of emotional states such as trauma, depression, fear, obsessive thinking, inertia, and others. I am sure the most popular and well-known essence is Rescue Remedy, used in any kind of traumatic or emergency or stressful situation. It is actually a composite of five flowers (Star of Bethlehem for shock, Cherry Plum for the feeling of loss of control, Rock Rose for fear and panic, Clematis for a sense of disconnection, and Impatiens as above). I have prescribed it for children who fell down while running, relatives after car accidents, a dog traumatized after surgery, and patients who received bad news. It can also be used in the process of psychotherapy to help take the edge off a difficult session or a time period in therapy when the memories coming up are too traumatic or when the emotions are too overwhelming. Rescue Remedy has been extremely helpful in my practice, and I suggest you try it and allow it to help you and your family.

I will often begin treatment using flower essences because they are so gentle. People seem to trust them, and I have seen very few adverse reactions. Flower essences are available over the counter, are inexpensive to use, and, like anything else in medicine, work better in the hands of experienced healers for complicated situations.

Having discussed physical health and energy medicine, let's move on to a subject close to my heart—peace of mind. Peace of mind involves refining our emotions and our intellect. Too often we find ourselves stuck in an old pattern of thinking and feeling. These dysfunctional mental habits may be accompanied by a restrictive philosophy of life that prevents us from feeling safe, balanced, and fulfilled. Let's explore this mental/spiritual realm and learn how to be present in the moment with our adult capabilities, and learn an uplifting perspective on life so that we may enjoy the adventure of life and grow in an upward direction.

Part Three

Peace of Mind

From "Lost to Found"

WHAT IS PEACE of mind? There are probably many definitions. As I look back on the various periods of training and experiences of my life, I realize that I had not only acquired some degree of physical health but also an understanding of how to "be" in the world and my place in it. I believe that there were two major influences that helped me go from lost to found, so to speak, from confused and searching to purposeful living.

The first one, psychotherapy, discussed in chapter 15, has to do with removing emotional dysfunction that quite literally keeps us tied to the past in an unhappy way and consequently blocks our upward development. The discussion includes an example of couples counseling where each individual learns to befriend his or her inner child. I also talk about the importance of the flight or fight response and how we can manage it in a positive way. In chapter 16, I discuss the second major influence that affected me: the concept of divine providence, that there is a divine plan for each and every one of us, and how that plan guides us to our personal soul correction and helps us to fulfill our unique purpose in life. Allow me to explain.

15

The Power of Psychotherapy

Removing Old Ties that Bind

Some of us are not free to express our true opinions, beliefs, and creativity. I'm talking about when something or someone presents itself to us in our environment and we react in a reflexive way, rather than a truthful way. Why?

This is because we are burdened from "old ties that bind" so that we are not free to experience the world as it really is; rather, we experience it through the lens of our personal past history. We may even have a sense of our inability to act freely yet feel unable to do anything about it. As a first step to having peace of mind, we need to free ourselves from these old reflexive patterns. A powerful tool for this is psychotherapy.

Here is an example of how it works. The following story is a representation of many people over the years I have had the privilege to help. The details have been changed to protect privacy so that this example does not refer to any specific couple yet retains the ability to demonstrate what I'm trying to show you. If you can identify a little with this couple or parts of their story, my hope is you may be able to benefit and learn how to free yourself from a situation that needs to change for the better in your own life.

An Unhappy Marriage

A forty-year-old woman, Mrs. Blue, and her forty-five-year-old husband are struggling in their marriage. They feel depressed. They are having difficulty speaking to each other about anything significant.

Let me give you a little history. Mr. Blue is stressed in his job and is worried about making a living. His wife works part time and also is home, taking care of their two children. When they talk together, he appears very opinionated and aggressive and talks as if his way is the "right" way. He is physically large and when frustrated can appear physically intimidating. His wife is smaller, speaks softly, and, while every bit as intelligent as him, has difficulty holding her own in the conversation.

He "presses her invalidation button."

This is what happens. In discussions together, he tends to assert himself in a "my way is the right way" attitude. When she stands up for what she believes, he becomes verbally aggressive. Her reaction? She feels belittled, unsupported, and put down as if her opinions do not matter. We call this sequence of events "pressing her invalidation button." Everyone has his or her own unique button. She then backs off and allows herself to be steamrolled because she feels intimidated, and, at the same time, she harbors a fear that he might abandon her if she really held her own. Withdrawing into herself, she despairs of being heard or taken seriously and becomes depressed.

She "presses his abandonment button."

As she withdraws, Mr. Blue reacts with anger because he, in turn, feels abandoned by her, which soon yields to his feeling depressed. In this marriage, this kind of communication has repeated itself over and over throughout the years. In general, when someone's "button" gets pressed, it triggers his or her locked-in emotional reflexivity from the past that prevents the person from expressing his or her truth in the here and now.

I think of this as metaphorically stepping into a "bear trap." Why? It consists of an old memory, conflict, behavioral pattern, or habit that locks on to the person's psyche when his or her button is pushed. Think of it this way. Just like when you are in an elevator and someone pushes the down button and you go down, here, you are going along, living life, and someone or some event triggers your vulnerable button, and down you go, experiencing the dysfunctional ties that bind you to the past with all the thoughts and feelings that accompany it.

The Emancipation of Mrs. Blue

During talk therapy, we discovered some very important things, and these discoveries led to insight, which led to change! The first major realization was that in some ways, the couple actually resembled each other's parents. Let's look at this first through the eyes of Mrs. Blue.

"My husband reminds me of my father," she exclaims in a surprised voice. Mrs. Blue recalls that her father was a large man and very serious. He had to have his way around the house. He was the boss, and the others in the house tiptoed around him. If she had a difference of opinion or disagreed about something, he would become angry and dominate her, and she would feel small and insignificant. And naturally, as his daughter, she loved him and was afraid to lose his love. In her family, she was one of many children, and coming along later in the birth order meant that in this family, her opinion was neglected and ignored. Everyone knew more than she did because they were older, and her experience was that her opinion didn't really matter. She remembers the pain as emptiness and recalls feeling "I'm just an afterthought." Ouch.

Reliving Her Childhood

As therapy continued, much to her surprise, we discovered that she was reliving the experience of childhood in her marriage! Every time she would argue with her husband, an unconscious hand would reach up from her past and transform her perspective of her loving husband into a "father-figure" husband. She would "relive" her childhood all over again in the present moment, and, right there and then, become that helpless little girl, disrespected, ignored, unimportant, and feeling like "I'm a nothing, a nobody." All this while she was talking with her husband in her adult, grown-up body. It's as if you're walking along the path of life, and all of a sudden, an event, memory, sensation, conversation, or even a glance from someone triggers your button, and you step into a metaphorical bear trap that clamps down on you, keeping its hold on you. It won't let you go and pulls you down, down into the memories, feelings, and thoughts of childhood.

Protecting Her Inner Child

After some time in therapy, the realization of this pressing-the-button-getting-caught-in-a-bear-trap process settled in. How to help her?

We set about teaching her tools to "update" the situation so that she no longer emotionally confused her husband with her father, and she no longer would do this with any authority figure again. This understanding helped her see why she felt unimportant and helpless and feared abandonment when confronting her husband—because she remembers that's exactly how she felt as a little girl at age seven. She was actually regressing to her little-girl state in those marital conversations. She looked forty but was emotionally seven. Wow.

It took a while as the impact of that understanding sank in. She had to grasp the idea that her adult woman needed to emerge and protect that psychological part of her mind we call the "inner child" and assert herself as the adult woman and not lose herself.

"Losing herself" took place every time her button was pressed. Pressing the button meant the disappearance of her adult psychological self as she emotionally slid down from the present to the past, and there she was, the inner child, left all alone (without her adult self), trying to cope with her father's demands as in the above example, or cope with any other "button-pushers" who come along, like a boss, a relative, etc., who trigger the same response.

This is inappropriate and impossible. Why? The inner-child part of us is not made to handle adult responsibilities. Please understand this. These childlike parts of our inner psychological selves need the love, guidance, and reassurance of our more mature adult psychological selves. How do we accomplish this?

Practice Really Helps

In her case, we taught a simple technique combined with homework assignments so that she could practice staying present in her adult self in any situation. And this is indeed what she did. Over a period of time and with much practice, she learned how to stand her ground. Now in conversations with her husband, she refused to regress to that little-girl state, stood her ground as an adult woman, and was willing to take the consequences of a give-and-take relationship. She saw clearly how he and others would press her button, painfully sending her down the elevator to "childhood," and she refused to let that happen.

As you can imagine, the taste of adulthood within the marital dyad became emancipating. As therapy continued, she reported how she would be fine and then begin to slip down the path toward childhood, followed by the struggle to right herself. This happened over and over again.

As you know, they say that "practice (the correct way) makes perfect." Over time, she felt more consistently her adult self and more capable about the challenge of improving her marriage, and she wanted to give it a good try. Did she free up the "ties that bind" her to the past? As you know, nothing is perfect, but she has essentially freed herself from an emotional "straightjacket" that limited her creativity and bound her in darkness to the past. She now feels free and unencumbered to negotiate the necessary challenges that we all face from an adult (not a child) perspective.

But what of her husband? I believe that the vehicle of marriage is a remedy for two souls to heal, and that most of the time, spouses have equal representation in all that's good and bad. Let's look at his side of things.

His Story—Neglect and Humiliation

Mr. Blue told me that he grew up in a family with an absent father and a loving yet uncommunicative mother. Large for his age, he described himself as a "fat, slow, stupid kid," and was actually held back from passing into third grade. He remembers this as "flunking second grade." He recalls wearing clothing that were hand-me-downs, were out of style, and didn't fit him. He remembered feeling embarrassed and ashamed by his size, awkwardness, inappropriate and misfitting clothing, and lack of ability in school. He feared humiliation and rejection by the other kids on a daily basis.

When I gently asked him to associate these memories and feelings to an age, he answered "somewhere between ten and fourteen." This kind of childhood experience translated into the following adult ideation: "I'm nothing unless I can have riches. I only exist if I am 'somebody.' I can't afford to fail. If I lose money, or if I'm wrong about something, I fall into the 'bear trap' of 'I'm a nobody,' and I descend to the pits of humiliation, self-loathing, loneliness, and despair that I felt as a child. If my opinion is respected as correct or my financial picture is bright, I maintain a sense of self and a sense of dignity, and I can live with myself."

Does his plight sound familiar? Many men in the primary provider role of a family have a similar storyline. There are variations on the same theme: qualified love. I'm only OK if I produce wealth, I'm good-looking, I'm dressed a certain way, people like me, or I'm educated. The list is endless.

Rescuing His Inner Child

To help him, I engaged him in psychotherapy, and we followed a similar approach as that of his wife. As in her case, our goal was to make him aware of his button. We pointed out that during his conversation with her, if she said something that unconsciously pressed his button, he would suddenly regress to an early emotional age and experience the event from his inner child. We explained that when this happens, if you were to look at him from the outside, he appears as an adult. If you could see inside his mind at that moment, you would see a child aged ten to fourteen. His personal challenge became a quest to understand and experience in the present moment that his wife having her own opinion was not humiliating or rejecting him, and indeed, he had grown up into an articulate, attractive, and valued man!

If he could maintain his adult identity and not regress to childhood, he could hold his own in the conversation without being threatened and let his wife speak and contribute as well. This dynamic became the focus of his personal growth, and after a while, he was able to figuratively put up a Do Not Disturb sign on his button, which made it easier to maintain his adult self. As for the couple being their own entity, the challenge was to have them come back together again and reintegrate as two adults. Let's reexamine their interaction from the point of view of a before-and-after picture.

Understanding and Integration

Pressing the button, falling into the bear trap, and here we go all over again!

Let's reexamine their habitual interaction using the terms we have learned. An issue comes up for discussion, and the couple begins a dialogue. He expresses his opinion (secretly needing to be right to maintain a sense of self-esteem). She expresses a different opinion. Bingo! Her opinion has pressed his "disrespect button," or you can think of it as him stepping into his bear trap, and he begins to unconsciously feel those old feelings of failure and shame from childhood. He actually feels about seven years old. He responds by raising his voice and becoming critical with his words and defending his opinion.

This triggers her own bear trap from childhood as her father/family memories unconsciously jump to the fore to create in her a sense of invalidation and unimportance. She feels that "whatever I say doesn't matter, and I don't even exist," reliving her age from seven to twelve. At this point she withdraws emotionally to protect herself from her husband's attack and begins to feel depressed. Now he experiences the withdrawal of her love and attention as the very humiliation and rejection he was trying to avoid from the past. He quickly shuts down, becoming the depressed little boy.

This is the marital situation that repeats itself anytime Mr. and Mrs. Blue try to discuss something that needs working through. These are the unconscious reflexive patterns of behavior that sit silently in their marital life awaiting the right opportunity to emerge and destroy any meaningful growth-oriented working through for the couple. However, now that we understand the problem, we can go about finding a solution.

Rectification of a Marriage

Pressing the button activates the flight or fight response. They begin their conversation. He speaks his mind, and she speaks hers. Immediately it is important to intervene before his button gets pushed and he feels challenged and begins verbally attacking. Therefore, I stop the conversation and ask him to focus on his breath. Why? I want to stop his "fight-or-flight" response from taking over his whole physiology, and I do this by giving him a simple command to breathe. What's happening here?

The Fight or Flight Response

Did you know that the body has a specific nervous system designed to protect us? It's called the "autonomic nervous system," consisting of the sympathetic and parasympathetic parts, and they work together like a teeter-totter. (See figure 15-1.)

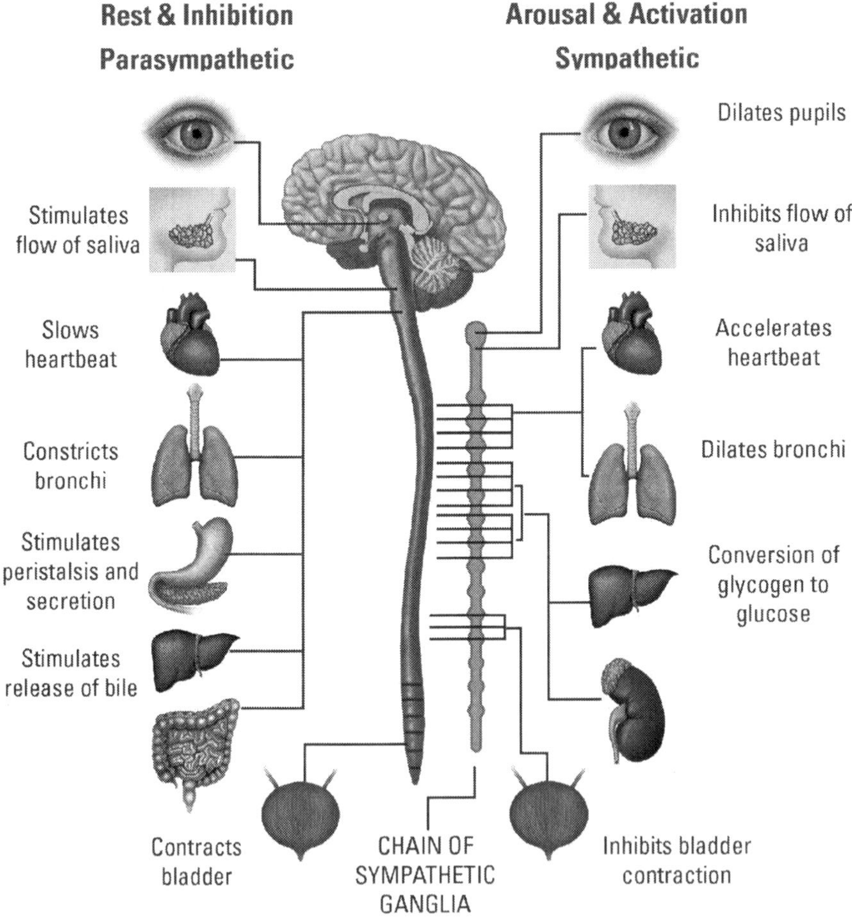

Figure 15-1. Autonomic nervous system.

On one hand, if danger is perceived, the sympathetic part of our nervous system automatically kicks in and enables us to defend ourselves or run for our lives. This is called the fight- or-flight response. The body does this by:

1. Directing more sugar and fats to enter the bloodstream to provide fuel for quick energy
2. Increasing the heart rate and blood pressure to get more oxygen to the cells in a hurry
3. Activating blood-clotting mechanisms to protect against bleeding from an injury
4. Increasing our muscle tone so that we can fight or run away
5. Shutting down digestion so that blood is diverted from our organs of digestion to the muscles of action

In my opinion, a shift takes place in brain functioning and consciousness. This shift moves the emphasis from our prefrontal lobe involved with human abstract thinking and planning to the midbrain—the amygdala, concerned with the animal emotions of survival such as fear and rage. How does this affect us? We now *react* to what's in front of us rather than *think* about what's in front of us because our animal mode has become dominant.

At this point in time,

- Our animal side dominates.
- The tail is wagging the dog.
- The amygdala is wagging the prefrontal cortex.

On the other hand, the parasympathetic mode promotes relaxation as the body does the opposite by:

1. Slowing the breathing and heart rate
2. Lowering the blood pressure
3. Lowering muscle tension
4. Restoring digestion
5. Shifting one's consciousness back to a less reflexive and more thinking and discriminating mode of functioning

As you can see, in an emergency, we are designed to react with the animal part of ourselves to save ourselves from danger. All well and good if we're in the jungle but not good just because your wife or another authority figure has his or her own opinion, which presses your button and activates your bear trap, and suddenly, your body is ready to fight or run away. Some describe a third mode called the freeze response resembling the response of a deer caught in the headlights.

In my years of experience, I'm convinced that what is described above is exactly what happens to a person. Something such as hearing bad news or someone raising his or her voice presses the person's button, and whoosh! He or she goes into a fight-or-flight response right there and then.

Breathing Restores Our Higher Self

As you might guess, the therapeutic implications of this phenomenon are huge. It becomes very important to train the patient to remember this fact: *The conscious act of focusing on your breath can downregulate the sympathetic part of the autonomic nervous system and lower the flight or fight response and upregulate the parasympathetic part, which promotes rest and calm.*

This stops the "tail from wagging the dog" and thereby stops the animal-oriented survival self from dominating the human self—just from breathing! Now let's return to Mr. and Mrs. Blue and observe the situation.

As they are talking to each other, we have just intervened with Mr. Blue, trying to short-circuit this animal response when his button is being pushed by asking him to breathe. While consciously breathing, he can hear her response without slipping into his past. He does not respond critically. He responds thoughtfully and with inclusiveness. She, in turn, now feels that her opinion is heard, and she is taken seriously and thereby avoids slipping down the slippery slope of childhood invalidation and unimportance. Behaviorally, Mrs. Blue avoids the need to protect herself and withdraw, and they both remain present in the moment and engaged with each other in the give-and-take of the conversation, which will lead to the next creative step in their lives. Hurray!

Freedom from a Burdensome Past

The therapy process helps us unburden ourselves from a heavy weight. What is this weight? It is the deep, unconscious, and unwanted connection that we have to the past that binds us to reflexive and repetitive responses in our work, personal relationships, and creative life. Therapy can remove this burden by creating freedom from the past that, in turn, helps us feel free to be in the moment with our creative, authentic selves. In the therapy process, we typically use many tools to accomplish this task. Here, I have highlighted the tools of breathing, remembering, and understanding.

Focused Breathing Can Stop the Crisis Mode

Breathing deliberately and consciously, as opposed to unconsciously, greatly affects your body/mind. The simple act of directing your attention to the flow of your breath has the astounding effect of slowing down the sympathetic nervous system and stimulating the parasympathetic nervous system.

As stated above, this slows down the body's crisis mode and keeps us out of the fight-or-flight response, thereby decreasing the animalistic, emotional response of rage or fear that overwhelms the mind's ability to think through things. Gratefully, using breathing, the teeter-totter swings the other way, relaxing the body/mind and shifting our consciousness into a human psychological/spiritual mode of functioning we call the "higher intellect." Now, instead of blindly reacting, the person can think. The person can remember.

Remembering Allows Understanding

Recalling the past resembles turning on a light bulb in a dark room and being able to see. Strong and original emotions often accompany remembering. These can be frightening because they are usually remembered from the small and helpless vantage point (perspective) of our inner child. That's why they are tucked away in the unconscious, because who would want to feel those helpless, angry, fearful, lonely feelings all over again? Nevertheless, they do exist.

They exert their strong influences on our daily interactions, day in and day out, with very little possibility of spontaneously changing. What to do about them? We have to process these memories and emotions of shame, pain, fear, rage, and even love, into the light of the here and now. I call this "updating" because it involves working through and integrating our past experiences into an adult understanding of the present. The remembering allows us the opportunity of seeing and reexperiencing the original trauma, with its associated feelings, such as pain or fear, in the eyes of our adult perspective. As we work together, the light bulb of understanding goes on over and over again. How? Each time an incident occurs, the individual catches himself or herself when beginning to slide back. He or she breathes, stops the fight-or-flight response, and retains his or her adult perspective. In the jargon of psychology, this process is called "working through" the issues. In the jargon of yoga, this process involves restoring the "higher intellect" mode of functioning, and I will go into more detail about that part of our mind in chapter 17.

Working toward a New Healthier Reality

Working through takes time as the past is integrated into the present, the child with the adult. A process of slow internalization of the new reality takes hold. This leads to deep understanding and real personal growth. The result is a weakening of the old reflexes, allowing new choices and promoting new behaviors and new responses. All this creates a little bit of a new you.

The sages of the past knew of this process. The yogis explained the power of understanding leading to change with this metaphor. Picture a sturdy coiled rope about three feet high. Now imagine the rope is burned with a flash fire. What's left? Does the rope still exist? The coiled rope is still there but as ash. Its form is unchanged, but it's a shadow of itself because its substance has changed, and it can no longer function as a rope.

The same holds true for our mind. We have flashes of insight that lead to new behaviors. When we remember an unpleasant event from childhood, work with it using the "higher intellect" part of our mind, and bring it into the "light" of understanding of adulthood, we transform it and break the power of this old mental pattern over us. It becomes a shadow of its old self, and its hold on us is broken. We become less encumbered by this past conflict and free to be present to the moment and think, speak, and act creatively and truthfully. This therapeutic process contributes to one's peace of mind as old rigid patterns of behavior are loosened up and are now relics or shadows of the past having lost their grip over you. The new you is empowered and feels a sense of expansion and freedom. I believe this ridding ourselves of ties that bind us to the past in a dysfunctional way is a first and major step toward having peace of mind.

The Next Step

At this point, unencumbered by the psychology of the past, I could now awaken each day feeling free and living in the present, but now I had to answer the question, what to do with my life? To answer this question, I needed to find a philosophy or belief system that integrated my personal and work life with my body/mind and with something greater. I had experienced the work of psychotherapy as a student, patient, and professional, but something was missing. I needed something to pull it all together. I needed to find a bigger picture and my role in it in order to feel peace of mind and feel complete.

16

Discover Divine Providence

I Am Not Alone

ONE DAY AS I talked to my teacher, I was feeling the pressures of the challenges of life, and I expressed my anxiety about how everything would work out. He looked at me and said, "You're not alone. There is a divine plan for you." I stopped in my tracks as I let the words sink in. A divine plan for me—a cosmic order, which included me and the personal and professional struggles I was facing, an overriding consciousness that watched over me and carefully orchestrated my reality. Really?

Think of it this way. A parent is watching over her child. The child plays, falls down, picks himself or herself up, uses crayons, gets messy, drinks, spills water, and safely lives in a space that is thoughtfully and lovingly provided by the parent. Everything in the space is watched over and provided by his or her mother in order for the child to live and grow, even as the child struggles through their age-appropriate challenges, blissfully unaware of mother's abiding vigilance and attention to her child's every need.

"Can this be true for me?" I wondered—an abiding and benevolent Spirit watching over me and orchestrating my challenges. That thought relaxed me. In this big world with seemingly unending levels of complexity where anything could happen, I was not alone. Something or someone was watching over me. These thoughts were the beginning of a very personal spirituality.

Life as Growth

What are the implications of living with a divine plan? My teacher said we are expected to grow by embracing the challenges that come along in our lives and work with them. We are given divinely orchestrated opportunities to improve ourselves and simultaneously change the world around us for the better. He said to think of the day as a *sadhana*—a spiritual practice. Grow as a human being. You know, make lemonade out of lemons!

If someone cuts in front of you on the expressway, instead of becoming angry and controlled by the flight or fight response that we spoke about above, you breathe and then deliberately think, "He is in a hurry because he is on the way to the hospital." Whoa. What has happened here? Your mind has used the situation to defuse nasty thoughts, feelings, speech, and maybe even a reckless reaction. Instead, you have judged someone favorably and elevated the situation with your thoughts, and you ended up a little more human, having created a sip of emotional lemonade! This little (but difficult) action contributes to what some call a "soul correction." Ancient wisdom from different traditions tells us that our entire purpose in life is to achieve a soul correction.

Soul Correction

Let me repeat, because I feel that this is a showstopper. We are here, on this earth, in this incarnation, in this family, with these friends, in this job, in this car, and going down this particular road at this particular time—all for a soul correction to heal our souls! I'm flabbergasted and love the idea. It's new and has a déjà-vu feeling all at the same time. Everything begins to fall into place, and I feel less confused about why I am alive. I am alive to correct or rectify some aspect of my soul life, and I'm using the physical world as the vehicle to do it.

Our Unique Purpose in Life

Even more, the sages insist that each soul is unique. Your soul has a unique purpose to fulfill during this lifetime. They say that if your unique soul does not fulfill the tasks that were meant for it, the general work of creation will go unfinished until the end of time and more specifically, so will your own soul correction. Think of creation as a giant unfinished puzzle. We individual souls fill in our piece of the creation puzzle by how we live our lives. Each of us has a unique piece to place in the finished work, and if we do not fulfill our purpose in life, that piece of the puzzle (our particular soul contribution) never gets added, and the puzzle remains incomplete forever!

Every time I think about this idea, I feel inspired and very special because of my uniqueness, and I feel charged with a mission, a life mission. Can this be the "adventure" of life that I have been seeking? A lot is going on here. In my personal life, there is a daily adventure that involves accepting the events and challenges that come my way and working with them so that I grow as a human being. And that's not all.

World Correction

At the same time as we work with these events and mold our thoughts, speech, and actions to improve ourselves, we also help "fix" the world we live in. This is called a "world correction" or *tikkun olam* (in Hebrew, meaning "repairing or healing the world"). For example, I take it upon myself to smile at someone (because that is difficult for me to do), and he smiles back. I feel better, and now I more easily smile at the next two people I see, and they smile and act friendly. The world now has four smiling people acting friendly and is probably a better place for it. This is a *tikkun olam* because we have brought a little healing to the world that wasn't there before. Now all we have to do is add the instigating and guiding influence of Spirit, and we have a more complete picture. (See figure 16-1.)

A Spirtual Bargain

PURPOSE IN LIFE

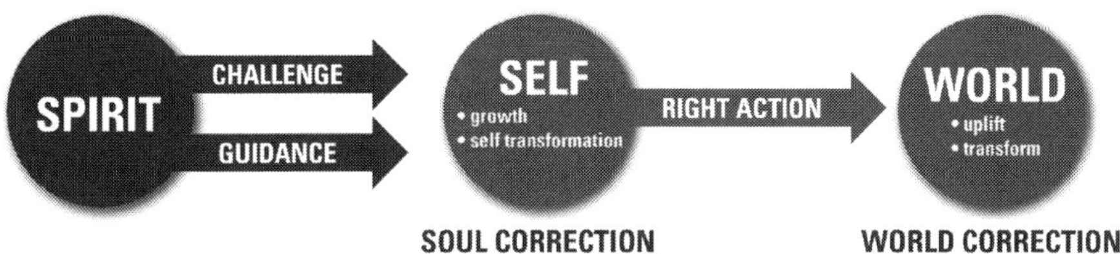

Purpose: Use our personal challenges to transform ourselves, perform right actions and thereby spiritualize, uplift, and transform the world around us.

Figure 16-1. Purpose in life.

The figure shows the following: There is a divine plan for you. That plan includes specific trials, tribulations, events, and opportunities (labeled above as "challenge") designed by providence specifically for your soul growth. This happens continually throughout life. This is life. And thankfully you are not alone in working with these challenges/opportunities because there is also help and guidance provided from above that you can tap into with training and intuition (more about that in the next chapter). Now as you proceed to work through the event and do the right thing called for, over time and with repetition, you change yourself and become a better person. This is called a "soul correction." The "right actions" that come from the "improved" you help change the world for the better. This is called a "world correction." Two for one! What a spiritual bargain, because you're healing yourself and healing the world at the same time.

Some Examples

You're tired, but you walk the dog anyway (soul correction). On the walk, you say hello to a neighbor, the conversation lifts her spirits (world correction), and upon returning home, you feel good inside. You go out of your way to drop off a friend (soul correction), and when you get home, you think it was the best thing you did all day. You stretched your generosity to give a little extra bonus to your employee (soul correction), who can now afford her babysitter (world correction). You give a gift to the needy child down the street whose smile and sincere appreciation lights up your heart. You give the lecture even though you're scared (soul correction of working through your fear), and at the end, someone comes up and thanks you for inspiring them to begin an organization around that very idea (someone and something has changed in the world for the better). You take time off from work to drive your child the long way to school. On the way, you stop and eat, see a few sights, tell stories, share personal issues, and meet some lovely people on the road (world correction). The bonding and appreciation between you and your child are unexpected and fulfilling (soul and world correction). The list of examples goes on and on because the opportunities are as endless as souls needing corrections on this earth.

Peace, Purpose, and Fulfillment

Working through the ties that bind us to the past allows us a sense of freedom and a sense of lightness of being. We are free to live and respond in the here and now and not remain obligated to a fixed, reflexive, and often negative behavior that really blocks our true creativity from coming out. Adding a philosophy of life that includes thinking of life as a spiritual practice adds direction and focus to life that includes depth of meaning, purpose, and fulfillment. The lightness of being and creative potential we have acquired through therapy can now be focused when we awaken each morning into a world that will challenge us to grow internally, creating our personal *tikkun*, and simultaneously challenge us to make the external world a better place to live, a world *tikkun.* Found versus lost, guided versus abandoned, fulfilled versus empty, and focused versus endless wandering. Good-bye, confusion. Hello, deep satisfaction from a satisfying life.

Now that we have a model for physical health and peace of mind, let's take the next step on the rung of the ladder pointed up and explore a subject I call "clarity of consciousness." This involves creating a partnership between our body/mind and spirit and being able to use that partnership for something really wonderful—nothing less than changing ourselves and uplifting the world around us in which we live.

Part Four

Clarity of Consciousness

What Is Clarity of Consciousness?

When I speak of this, I refer to a state of mind in which a person is outwardly awake, alert, and aware of the external environment, and inwardly, he or she is open to his or her internal experience yet free from distracting thoughts and emotions. It is a state of heightened awareness, yet the person is relaxed and fully functional.

I think of this clarity as our ability to be conscious of something higher while simultaneously living in the physical everyday world of work, family, and recreation. How to achieve this? In chapter 17, I explore the faculty of intuition and introduce a yoga model of the mind in order to give us an intellectual framework for bridging the physical with the spiritual. In chapter 18, I review the power of breathing and its effects on our physical, energetic, mental, and spiritual levels of functioning. In chapter 19, I discuss the how and why of meditation as a path to clarity of consciousness followed by meditation's effects on our four levels of functioning as well as a discussion about how meditation helps us change for the better. The chapter ends with a discussion about soul correction and purpose in life. In chapter 20, I provide a brief summary by pulling together the concepts of the book as we attempt to "become the instrument."

17

Develop Personal Spiritual Sensitivity

The Hidden Jewel of Intuition

THE HIGHER INTELLECT we mentioned in chapter 15 (see figure 17-1) plays a key role in this state. I think of this consciousness as a heightened "soul availability," where the person is connected to his or her higher spiritual self while remaining in the world of action. Some people call this "meditation in action" because they use a higher type of consciousness, often associated with the meditative state, and simultaneously apply that to their thoughts, feelings, and actions as they live in the material world. This is the meeting place where the finite of the physical world meets the infinite of the spiritual world. As a physician, I have been trained to default to this position for listening to and helping others. Why is this a good thing, and how does this work?

A Yoga Model of the Mind

The "higher intellect" part of our mind serves as a channel to connect two apparently separate modes of our existence. On one hand, it connects to our conscious and unconscious thoughts, feelings, and sense of personal identity as well as to the physical world of bodily sensations. On the other hand, it transcends the physical, revealed world, stretching up into the spiritual domain where divine knowledge reigns. (See figure 17-1.)

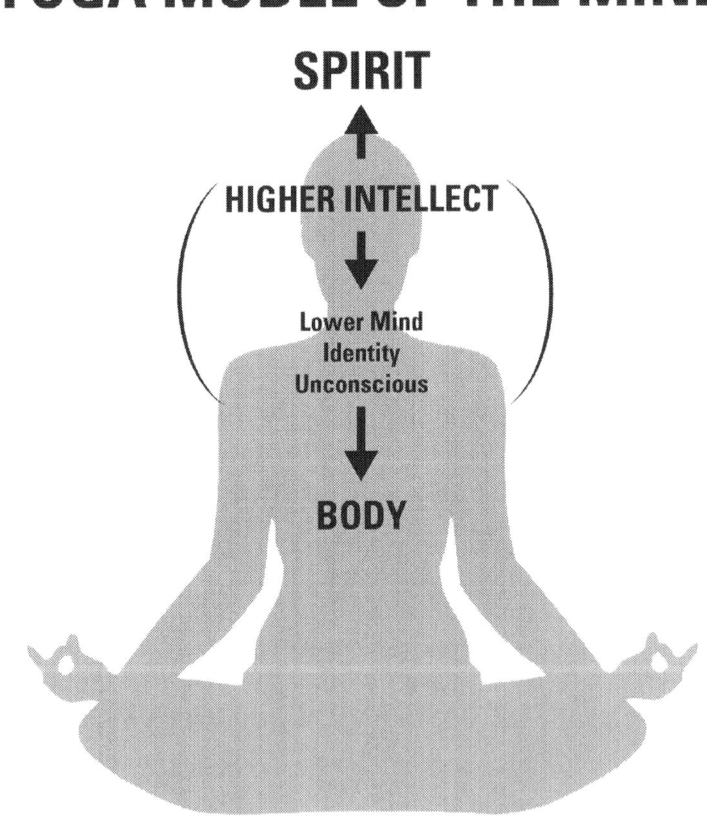

Figure 17-1. Yoga model of the mind.

Hence, we can and do tune in to the spiritual domain. When this happens, we often call this "intuition." Intuitions come quickly. In kabala it is referred to as the flash of insight (*chochma*) that comes from above. Common language refers to this phenomenon as a light bulb turning on, because "shedding light" on a situation, seeing, insight, and understandings are all related to each other. In those times when we have clarity of consciousness, I believe we become a *kali* or vessel for this blessed information to become revealed in our minds. Sounds good, but why is this important?

Come Closer to Divinity

It's important because being closer to divinity within and without presents us with an opportunity. What exactly is this opportunity? Think of it this way. We are very familiar with the physical domain such as eating food, experiencing objects, feeling our bodies, and sensing the natural world all around us. Some declare that this is all there is or that this is the most important part of existence. Others experience life as more interior and subtle to the physical, i.e., the spiritual world, and they feel that to be spiritual and rise above earthly existence is the final goal of a human. Traditions in yoga and Hassidism, however, teach that bringing the spiritual into the physical in order to elevate it, spiritualize it, and reveal the spiritual energy in it is the goal of humanity.

Bringing the Spiritual into the Physical

Let me repeat. Allowing ourselves to become a vessel or channel to bring divine knowledge down into our world and use it to help shape our thoughts, speech, and actions is a very good thing. How is this done? It can be as simple as saying a blessing (speech) over food (physical) and using the food for energy to live out your purpose that day. You could give money for charity to someone who is hungry, thus "elevating" the money by using it for a higher purpose. You can meet up with a difficult person and deliberately intention a loving interaction between you and him or her. This will change how you view that person and talk to him or her, thus elevating your speech and conversation. Think of the endless ways your interactions with people and objects in the physical world around you can be spiritualized, but the trick is to be conscious—to have clarity of consciousness along with the intention to take what life has to offer and elevate it. I call this practical spirituality.

How does one develop this skill? I expect there are many pathways. I want to focus on two techniques that I have found personally helpful to develop this clarity. First, I will discuss the effects of using breathing for clarity. Second, I will discuss the use of meditation.

18

Breathing as a Path to Clarity of Consciousness

Breathing is one of my favorite paths to clarity of consciousness. Recall the "sheaths of life" we spoke of earlier in the basic concepts section of part 1, chapter 3, when discussing *Sankhya* philosophy. *Sankhya* philosophy describes a larger view of human functioning, including the physical, energetic, mental, and spiritual parts of our makeup. We are amazingly complex and wondrous! Let's see how changing the way we breathe can affect all these levels, leading to a higher state of awareness.

How Breathing Affects Each Sheath

1. The Physical Sheath (Annamaya Kosha): Breathing Calms the Nervous System

In chapter 15 we demonstrated how to work with the breath in a therapy session. In the case of Mr. Blue, he used breathing to slow down his fight-or-flight response. Conscious, slow, and even breathing will downregulate the sympathetic nervous system and upregulate the parasympathetic nervous system, thereby calming the body. This is an example of using the breath to directly affect our nervous system and calm the body.

2. The Energy Sheath (Pranamaya Kosha): Breathing Balances Energy

Concerning the energy part of our being, we discussed several types of breathing in chapter 12. We mentioned that the "pre-meditative" breathing would balance the normally one-sided nostril dominance we find in daily activities. By working with this breathing technique, we can create a state of balance between both nostrils, which then creates a third energy pathway in the spine, called *sushumna* in yogic terminology. This balanced energy, previously unavailable, is now ready to travel upward and empower our minds for activities such as concentration, contemplation, prayer, and meditation.

3. The Mental Sheath (Manomaya Kosha): Breathing Promotes Mindfulness, Reduces Fear, and Establishes Emotional Clarity

In chapter 15 we discussed the mental/ emotional level. We mentioned that activating the fight-or-flight response is designed to protect us from danger. This response affects our minds as well as our bodies. When activated, it produces a stressful, fear-based emotional tone resembling animal-like consciousness.

Brain Chemistry—Human or Animal

This is accompanied by increased amygdala activity in the brain. The brain chemistry is complex. I want to mention a small piece of what scientists are thinking. The amygdala has been called the "fear center" because it is involved with emotions and memories related to fear and anxiety. Therefore, it's not surprising that stimulating the fight-or-flight response, accompanied by increased amygdala activity, results in the experience of an animal-like instinctual behavior and in a reflexive, reactive psychological feeling to any situation, i.e., acting before you think. The opposite is true when the fight-or-flight response is calmed down. How does this happen?

Located at the front of the brain, the prefrontal cortex is known for its "executive" function involving such functions as memory, reasoning, problem solving, and planning. There is speculation that prefrontal cortical activity, which is associated with higher reasoning, may help modulate and inhibit amygdala activity.[41]

Shifting Identity from Animal to Human

Therefore, I believe that we actively engage the prefrontal cortex part of our brain when we perform focused, conscious breathing to calm down the fight-or-flight response. I also feel that focused breathing promotes mindfulness, and this mindfulness allows for a shift in emotional identity away from our animal state. This shift goes along with promoting a humanlike experience involving thinking, conceptualizing, and abstraction (think before you act).

Breathing Restores Freedom to Choose

I want to repeat this for emphasis. When the animal, instinctual part of us takes over, we become overrun with neurological and chemical reactions that involuntarily immerse us in animal-like physicality. When we consciously regulate our breath, we stop and reverse that process and restore our higher functioning. We do this by promoting the mature, thought-out part of us. This may be accompanied by increased prefrontal cortical activity, which apparently inhibits the stress response in the amygdala, allowing for a consciously induced mindfulness, resulting in a sense of peace. Now we have identity. Now we have choice. Now we can experience those feelings without being buried by them. Now we can watch our thoughts and even work with them constructively and change them.

4. The Wisdom Sheath (Vijnanamaya Kosha): Breathing Connects the Body to the Soul

On the spiritual level, I experience something about the breath that is transcendental in an almost magical way and seems to be an almost effortless way to take the physical and spiritualize it. In the Bible we find that a humanlike creature becomes a "man" after the "breath of life" was breathed into him by G-d. The Hebrew word for breath is *neshima*, and the Hebrew word for soul is *neshama*. Notice how similar they are. These words come from the same etymological root. What does this teach us?

I believe that breathing connects the body to the soul; its roots are physical, and its reach is spiritual. Indeed, this is how I experience it. In my life, whenever I tune into my breathing, I immediately feel "in control" and centered. I observe the same results with my patients. When they are upset, I ask them to breathe. Immediately, they calm down, appear centered, and seem to connect to a higher part of themselves. This higher part provides them wisdom, support, and truth. Where does this higher self come from? I believe this is part of the soul that every human being has and all of us can connect to, instantly bringing us grounding, guidance, and a sense of timeless spirituality.

Summary

Breathing techniques are simple and easy to learn, take little time, and have profound effects on all parts of our body/mind. I'm a big fan of using breathing techniques on a daily basis. While breathing may be a convenient method for connecting to the spiritual parts of ourselves, I also admire meditation as another method offering clarity of consciousness and the possibility of a deep spiritual journey with lasting effects.

19

Meditation as a Path to Clarity of Consciousness

What Is Meditation?

I CONSIDER MEDITATION to be a spiritual exercise to develop skills and obtain experiences that bring goodness to the self and benefits to the world. Much is written about the subject, and I believe there is some confusion about the use of this word. When some people talk about meditating, they are really referring to the process of contemplation or concentration or even a personal conversation with G-d.

When I refer to meditation, I refer to a process that involves the mind mentally hearing a sound. The muscles of speech or vocalization are not used in any way. The sound is allowed to mentally repeat itself over and over as one focuses on the sound with his or her mind. This is referred to as mantra meditation because the word "mantra," in Sanskrit, means sound, word, or instrument of speech. The sound usually is a word taken from scriptures or a word or phrase suggested by those who are versed in the various schools and traditions of mantras from around the world.

Simple Steps to Begin Meditation

In beginning meditation, I suggest the following sequential steps.

1. Loosen and Relax the Body

Choose a quiet room with as few distractions as possible. Then gently stretch or do a few yoga postures to prepare the body to be able to sit for a period of time without pain or difficulty.

2. Establish a Position in Which to Meditate

It is important to establish a firm and stable sitting posture so that the body does not waver or become a distraction during the meditation. I recommend sitting upright in a chair, using the back of the chair for support, or sitting on one or two pillows with the legs folded in a square. The head, neck, and trunk are straight with an ascending energy while the rest of the body is relaxed. The hands may be resting on the knees or folded in the lap.

3. Regulate Your Breathing

The awareness is deliberately withdrawn from the external environment, and the mind is directed to flow with the flow of the breath. The breathing is stabilized using one of the techniques previously discussed. This is followed by establishing breath awareness at the nostrils as previously discussed in chapter 12, the premeditative breath.

4. Coordinate Breathing with Listening to an Internal Sound (Mantra)

The eyes are now closed as the person now focuses on a sound to the exclusion of all other stimuli. The person mentally hears the sound repeating itself over and over and is instructed to "mentally follow" the sound. This requires steady effort and concentration. In the beginning, the student's inhalation and exhalation are coordinated with the mental repetition of the sound. At later stages, the breath takes on its own rhythm as the student concentrates only on the sound and excludes all other sensations including the awareness of his or her own breathing.

5. Let Go of Unneeded Thoughts, Feelings, and Sensations

As the meditation progresses, the meditator is taught to avoid any distractions that would remove his or her focus from the sound because it is necessary to become aware of any impediments that block the mind's focus from following the sound. Therefore, we are taught to acknowledge and then dismiss or let go of the thoughts, ideas, feelings, or sensations as they come up into our awareness.

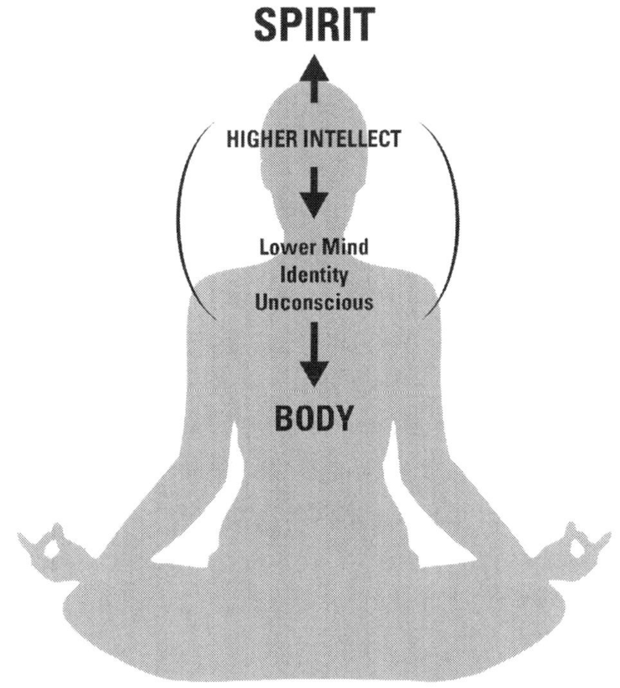

Figure 19-1.

For example, as the person is concentrating on the repeating mental sound, he or she may perceive sounds (real or imagined) or visions and must let them flow out of his or her consciousness and not dwell or think about them. The meditator may encounter thoughts. These thoughts (from the lower mind) may be from his or her daily routine such as unfinished tasks he or she must perform, or he or she may experience feelings coming up from the unconscious or memories from the past (*chitta*—unconscious mind). A whole story line may emerge with clarity and detail.

Again, the meditator's task is to let them go. Slowly and deliberately, the concentration on the sound folds into what we technically term meditation. At a deeper level of unfolding, the meditator encounters his or her sense of identity, the sense of "I-ness" that creates familiarity (*ahamkara*). This also can be let go.

6. Develop the Higher Intellect and Witness (Buddhi)

With practice, this steady concentration on the sound leads to a very focused awareness, what the yogis call a "one-pointed mind." This mindfulness becomes the vehicle and haven for observation as the meditator journeys through "degrees and grades" of consciousness. It is taught that the sound will "lead" the meditator to deeper levels of consciousness. The part of the mind that is focusing, observing, and doing the "letting go" is referred to as the higher intellect or witness or *buddhi*. This term is derived from the Sanskrit word *budh*, meaning, "to understand, to know." This part of our mind is said to have one part of itself connected into the body/mind awareness and another part of itself connected to the higher consciousness we will call spiritual. (See figure 19-1.)

Successful meditation strengthens and develops a laser-like one-pointed ability of the mind to focus and develop our higher intellect or "witness." The witness discriminates and discerns. It is the spaceship connecting the dimensions across time and space. It has one foot in the material world of body, perception, feelings, thoughts, and identity, and the other foot in the spiritual domain of intuition and beyond. *Buddhi* listens to the information coming down from the spiritual world and passes that down and processes it into feelings and thoughts that the other parts of the mind can use for everyday guidance.

This *buddhi*-guided behavior is actually spiritually guided activity. Some call this "meditation in action." Here lies the potential of meditation for helping us in our quest to spiritualize and uplift the physical world around us by bringing the spiritual to the physical and literally enlighten our minds with the light of the higher worlds. Over time, the practice of meditation is said to build the "muscle" of *buddhi*, resulting in this powerful tool for mindfulness being available to help you live your daily life.

I find this technique encourages the disciplined study of consciousness in a safe, personal, and creative way. Find yourself a qualified teacher or guide, especially when you are in the beginning stages of meditation.

Why Meditate? (How Does Meditation Affect Our "Sheaths"?)

Allow me again to refer back to our concept of "sheaths of life" as described in *Sankhya* philosophy in chapter 3. We will use the sheaths as steps ascending the ladder of physical, mental, and spiritual health and growth in our quest to understand meditation.

1. The Physical Sheath

Over the years, science has worked with meditation, and studies have been done in many areas including meditation and its effect on pain management. Here, I want to focus briefly on a couple of conclusions that I share with patients often. A major finding is that decreasing the fight-or-flight response reduces some of the effects of stress. Using meditation, you can slow the heart rate, lower blood pressure, and reduce muscle tension. In my practice, I often recommend that patients who are diagnosed with hypertension use meditation as a technique to help regulate their blood pressure. I also recommend its use to help with medical conditions related to tense musculature such as tension headache. There are also beneficial effects on brain neurotransmitters that may positively affect your mood. Therefore,

I have prescribed breathing and meditation lessons for patients with symptoms of anxiety, and many of them have succeeded in lowering their everyday anxiety after learning and practicing these techniques.

2. The Mental Sheath and Mental Cleansing

During the meditation technique, you will mentally listen to the mantra repeating itself. You will notice a continuous flow of thoughts, feelings, memories, or images that present themselves and seem to distract your ability to concentrate on the sound. Why is this happening? Actually, there is a well-known pattern to these phenomena.

What is most superficial and recently recorded in the mind comes up first. This is followed by what is deeper and older, and finally what is in the deepest recesses of your mind. I think of this as a mental cleansing of all the stored information we have absorbed but may not really need. Let's use the example of a closet full of items that we have accumulated over a period of time. We clean it out by first going to the easy-to-reach shelves and removing unneeded things. Then we can reach the deeper, harder-to-get-to areas and clean those shelves, too.

Our mind works in a similar fashion. As we meditate and the pattern unfolds, we first observe what is known as the day residue. The day's amalgam of events, trials, and tribulations take their stage and then make their exit. A little anger here, a little worry there, and we let those thoughts go.

Going Deeper

Next up, we notice more subtle feelings and thoughts related to your life events, a face, a portion of a conversation—all to be let go during the process of concentrating on the sound. Then a deeper layer comes up from the sands of *chitta*, such as a word, a whisper, or an impression of love from the unconscious past. It could be the memory of a loved one, a painful good-bye, a regret about something left unsaid, or a desire to hold or be held. This unfolding makes for a beautiful and somewhat peaceful cleansing process as the meditator observes, acknowledges, and lets go of the stream of consciousness passing before his or her mind. The result? A sense of profound stillness—the feeling of "empty mind" resulting from a quieting of the mind that is both freeing and expansive.

3. Developing Discernment and Downloading Spiritual Information

But now that the mind has been "emptied," how does this help us? Think of this by way of analogy. Once a cup is empty, it can be filled. I think of this filling process in two ways. Firstly, an alert and open mind can sensitively receive accurate information horizontally from the world around us and use that information to improve our thoughts, speech, and actions in life. Secondly, our clear and alert mind can now vertically channel information from the spiritual realm above to below. This increased ability to discern the world around us and to "download" information from the spiritual world provides us with intuition, guidance, and a deeply personal sense of connection. These mindfully acquired skills are important gifts, enabling us not just to live and survive in the world but also to fulfill our purpose in life.

Changing Ourselves Using Meditation

The letting go of thoughts, feelings, memories, and subtle impressions during meditation can result in a changed person! How does this happen? How does change take place?

Change—Identification and Internalization

I see someone talking kindly, and I admire that. I identify with that person, and I model myself after that person by talking kindly to others. After a while, I am no longer imitating that person because I am naturally talking kindly to others on my own. I have "internalized" that behavior. It has become part of me, and I have changed for the better.

Change—Discovery and Working Through

Another path to change is "discovery and working through." In the case example of the couple in therapy (see chapter 15), the husband and wife each discovered that his or her rage and fear were conditioned reflexes from the past. They then proceeded, with help from the therapist, to understand their triggers and to recondition and free themselves from behaving in an automatic way. They changed themselves by understanding and "working through" their issues.

Change—Observing and Letting Go

In meditation, I think the predominant method promoting change is a process of "lightening up" and becoming more selfless with less "ego." For example, although a person may admit experiencing a feeling such as anger, one finds it difficult to control and continues to harbor it inside his or her mind. In meditation, "less is more"; therefore, the anger is processed differently. When meditating, the anger comes up into the awareness of the meditator and is observed by the observing part of the mind (higher intellect, witness, or *buddhi*) and then is consciously let go as the meditator returns to concentrating on the sound. (See figure 19-2.)

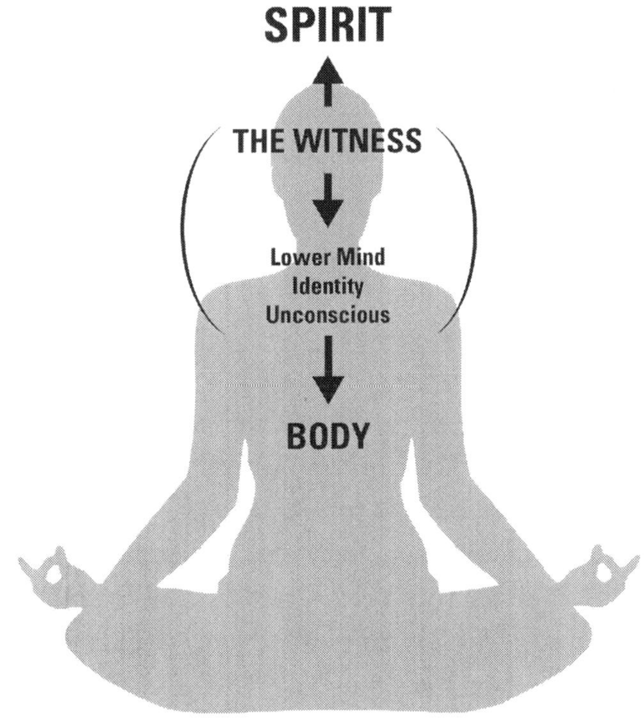

Figure 19-2. Letting go of emotion.

That piece of anger is now gone! The same can be said for letting go of grief, traumatic memories, doubt, fear, guilt, shame, and blame.

Negative Thoughts Are Like Rotten Food

In meditation, the gentle shedding of negative thoughts, feelings, and identifications results in a newer, cleaner, lighter, and more whole you. How does this result in more wholeness? Let's use the example of food. Rotten food may be mistakenly taken in and yet doesn't really become part of you. It has negativity, and the body tries to expel it, not incorporate it. The bad food was "introjected" but not "internalized" into who you are. Now let's turn to bad thoughts. They are considered "introjects," like foreign parasites that come in, hang on, and affect us negatively. They cannot become internalized as part of our psychic structure, however, because they are not healthy. Only loving, nurturing thoughts can become truly integrated into our body/mind. This bears repeating. We introject negativity. We put up with it, live with it, try to get rid of it, and sometimes unfortunately live with it all our lives. Yet it never really becomes part of us.

Cleansing the mind allows the soul to shine through.

On the other hand, good food is invited in, is needed, is metabolized, and quickly becomes part of us. Likewise, loving, nurturing experiences become part of us. We internalize and integrate them into our body/mind, and that's how we grow. Therefore, when we shed our unwanted "introjects," we are left with a more pure sense of self and a body/mind that feels more whole. It's like polishing a diamond. The process of meditation helps us to eliminate the impure, and what remains is pure. We are transforming ourselves by letting go of what is unneeded, resulting in a more refined sense of self where the soul can sparkle through.

The Spiritual Level—Intuition

As we continue to meditate, the mind clears out the day residue mentioned above and then proceeds to a deeper cleansing of the unconscious material that needs to express itself. At this point, the mind is "empty" of thoughts, and the meditator is experiencing clarity of consciousness. The observing part of our mind is now free to record information that seems to come from somewhere outside our mind.

Guidance from Above

Now we have a different opportunity. Suddenly, we may become aware of information that we had not previously known, and/or we see something in a different light that creates a flash of understanding that is completely new. Yoga tradition calls this layer of consciousness "intuition." Kabala tradition calls this *chochma*, a Hebrew word referring to that moment when a flash of insight is recorded by the mind. This intuition or insight is downloaded from above to below and makes its presence articulated in the "higher intellect," also known as the observer, witness, or *buddhi* part of our mind. (See 19-3.)

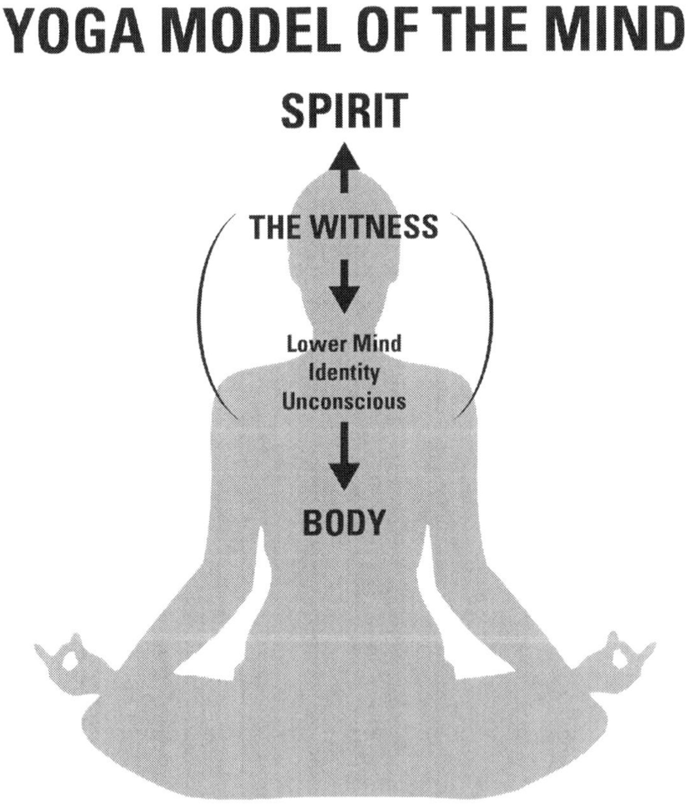

YOGA MODEL OF THE MIND

SPIRIT

THE WITNESS

Lower Mind
Identity
Unconscious

BODY

Figure 19-3. Connecting to intuition.

I have found that "guidance" literally pops into my consciousness in the way of ideas, insights, messages, and perspectives that turn out to be relevant to my life. Many times during morning meditation, a particular person will appear as a memory or a name, and I will let it go. Later that day, I find that very person on my schedule or meet that person in a store. As Yogi Berra, the famous New York Yankees catcher, once said, "It's like déjà vu all over again!" This is "spiritual sensitivity" to that which exists beyond time and space. But is this a good thing? Why do this? The answer is yes; it is a very good thing because I experience this as a practical way to connect to divine knowledge. It's as if a wonderful universal teacher is available and waiting for us to make ourselves available. Once we open, Spirit gives us information to "take back" to our everyday lives, helping us to live our day. All we need is a little spiritual sensitivity.

Spiritual Sensitivity—Looking Within

I believe there are many ways to develop this sensitivity, including contemplation and prayer as well as the clarity of consciousness brought by meditation. I consider meditation a nonreligious, practical method for connecting with that which is higher and greater than us. With clarity of consciousness, one naturally experiences spiritual sensitivity that allows us to look within.

This has a very practical application. At any time, we can center ourselves amid life's chaos and go to the calm within. It's as if we have an internal gyroscope that allows us to discover the "right next step" of our lives. Focusing on the right next step becomes an amazingly simple yet profound way to guide your life through the currents of life's questions and challenges.

Meditation in Action

Earlier, I mentioned the term "meditation in action." I referred to this as a term describing a type of consciousness, whereby a person takes his or her awareness often associated with the meditative state and simultaneously applies that to his or her thoughts, feelings, and actions while living in the material world. Every day we are faced with challenges that the traditions say are divinely tailored for each individual. Simultaneously, with clarity of consciousness, we can use our spiritual sensitivity to receive divinely inspired guidance for these everyday practical issues.

Some examples: What job should I take? Which school is best for my child? Do I stay in this relationship or not? Do I really have to make that call that I have been avoiding? Should I sleep some more or get up? In confronting my partner over a particular problem that we have to solve, do I use more unconditional love or tough love?

Purpose in Life—Our Soul Correction/World Correction

As you can see in figure 19-4, when we work through the issues that Spirit has placed in our path, we grow as humans and end up transforming the environment around us with our "spiritually" inspired actions. It's not easy, but the psychological struggles we work with and the spiritual practices we learn end up enabling us to change ourselves for the better. This is the "soul correction" part of our purpose in life.

Outwardly, our personal growth positively affects the things we say and the actions we do. These become the products of a partnership between the divine part of ourselves and the world around us.

These "right actions" can't help but spiritualize, uplift, and transform the world into a better place to live, thereby fulfilling a second goal of our purpose in life, that of world correction.

PURPOSE IN LIFE

SOUL CORRECTION **WORLD CORRECTION**

Purpose: Use our personal challenges to transform ourselves, perform right actions and thereby spiritualize, uplift, and transform the world around us.

Figure 19-4.

To summarize, our purpose in life is to take our divinely orchestrated personal challenges and use them to refine ourselves, perform right actions, and thereby spiritualize, uplift, and transform the world around us. Good stuff!

20

Becoming the Instrument

THE BASIC CONCEPTS that I have shared with you in part 1 served as a foundation of knowledge and provided me with the opportunity as a physician to reach specific goals both in patient care and my own health: that of physical health, peace of mind, and clarity of consciousness.

Physical Health

Physical health is bodily health. This is something we have to work for. As mentioned in the preface, we need to have a body that can support an active lifestyle of movement and physical productivity as well as mental and emotional growth. How to accomplish this?

I began by sharing some ideas about the "how" of eating consciously—how to think about food and how to actually eat the food. I followed with the topic of healthy food selection. This included a discussion about simple versus complex carbohydrates, proteins, good and bad fats, fruits, vegetables, and a "potpourri" of food entities, including vitamins, minerals, and foods to avoid. We then explored what the science of Ayurveda had to say about food therapy and body type, and we took a peek at the topic of herbs and botanicals that are used as medicines.

Bodily health requires movement. I first shared some important tips on how to exercise followed by a discussion on types of exercise and once again considered what the science of Ayurveda would recommend for your body type.

We concluded this topic of physical health by introducing the topic of energy medicine because the energy body is a transition between the physical and mental/emotional realm of existence and because energy medicine has great healing potential. After talking about my experiences with energy, I discussed its application for healing using breathing techniques, homeopathic therapeutics, and flower-essence therapy. I believe that food, exercise supplements, herbs, and energy medicine can help provide a person with a sound body.

Peace of Mind

This is a great gift. How can we accomplish this in our fast-paced modern life? I have shared with you two profound methods that have helped me settle into the world and find my place in it. The first method involved the use of psychotherapy. I have tried to demonstrate through a case study how our minds need to drop the old reflexive and dysfunctional behavior patterns that tie us down and bind us to the past, not allowing us to be fully present in the moment with all our adult capabilities. Once freed up of the ties that bind us to the past, we stand ready to live in the present moment with our energy enthusiasm and creativity.

The second method involves adding a spiritual perspective to our daily thinking, that of divine providence and its ramifications on our daily lives. What are these? First, know that we are not alone and that our challenges are tailor-made for our individual needs to grow. Second, this very personal growth leads to our "soul correction" and our actions help bring about a "world correction," and in this process, we come to realize that we have a unique purpose in life. This is an uplifting and comforting perspective helping us to relax and enjoy the adventure of life as we grow in an upward direction.

Clarity of Consciousness

With physical health, our bodies support us and serve as strong and energetic vehicles for our souls' earthly mission during the course of our lives.

With peace of mind, we are no longer trapped by old patterns of thought, speech, and action, and we are now free to develop in an upward direction. By adding an uplifting philosophy of life—that of divine providence—we take a comforting next step in climbing the ladder of spirituality.

With clarity of consciousness, we have the ability to turn inward and connect to our intuition within as we simultaneously live in the world without. I discussed two nonreligious and very practical methods: breathing and meditation. When we work with our breath in a conscious manner, we learn that breathing can calm our nervous system, balance our energy, promote mindfulness, and literally connect our body to our soul. When discussing meditation, we learned that meditation can relax the body and improve our health; cleanse our mind of unwanted, unneeded, toxic thoughts and feelings; "download" spiritual information into our intuition; and allow us to change unwanted and negative parts of ourselves. At this point, we have developed spiritual sensitivity—the ability to be conscious of something higher while simultaneously living in the physical everyday world of work and play.

Becoming the Instrument

As humans, we can utilize this spiritual sensitivity for the good and fulfill our unique potential for which we were created. We become a living channel, able to download information from above, and apply this to our purpose in life, which is to take our divinely orchestrated personal situations/challenges and use them to refine ourselves, perform right action, and thereby spiritualize, uplift, and transform the world around us.

This is the potential for Holistic Medicine.

Appendix 1

Suggestions for Living the Twenty-Four-Hour Day

Nighttime—Prepare to Sleep/the Day's Review

THE DAY ACTUALLY begins with the preparation the night before. First review the day's events and take note of anything that seems emotional or unfinished. Pay attention and "finish" the event by acknowledging that you felt sad at some news, or you were angry and held it in without expressing yourself, or you wanted to say "thank you" but lost the opportunity, or you felt loved by someone, and it was really nice. Why do this?

In the quietude of the night, when you're no longer occupied with the day's activities, the mind sees an opportunity to do something with all that unfinished emotional business accumulated from the day. All these unfinished thoughts and feelings and actions and desires may come up in your dream life as "day residue." The yogis say that we expend a lot of energy working out these issues, desires, melodramas, and conflicts in our dreams while we sleep. Therefore, a day review as described above can lead to their resolution and integration while we are awake. With the homework of the day done, a less busy and conflictual dream life will allow us to settle into a restful sleep.

Tomorrow's Plan

Others use this time to harness their powers of imagination and plan out what they want to have happen the next day. They may see themselves getting up at a certain time, followed by specific activities in the morning. Then they visualize what will happen in the afternoon concerning meetings, exercise, responsibilities, eating behaviors, etc. This practice is designed to help them accomplish their next day's goals.

Gratitude

Some traditions suggest the practice of giving gratitude whereby you express thankfulness for all the blessings that you have received during the day. You can do this as you go over the day review by looking for the positive in the way things turned out in your life that day, or you can do this as a separate practice. It can be for simple things that we take for granted, such as the car starting right up in the morning or the heat working during the winter. It might be more obvious to express gratitude for the more dramatic blessings that occur in our lives such as the new job offer that came our way or the wonderful person you just met or your child's achievement in life or hearing good news concerning a health-related issue. Gratitude leads to thankfulness and a feeling of love and humility. In the evening, humility feels right and is consistent with the feeling of surrender to something larger and good as you prepare to let go and sleep.

Morning—Awaken, Activate, and Cleanse

Upon awakening, give thanks that the soul is back in the body and then prepare for a little cleansing. First, begin a bowel cleanse with a traditional hot cup of water with a little honey, a pinch of salt, and a little lemon juice. This acts as a laxative as the honey is metabolized to Pitta (fire), the salt is Pitta, and the lemon is sour and astringent, which stimulates Pitta and Vata. These actions are mildly stimulating to the bowel. Drink this mixture quickly and follow it with this exercise. Gently squat on your toes and lower your right knee to the ground as you gently swivel slightly to the left. Then, return your right knee back to the starting position. Now gently swivel to the right and lower your left knee to the ground, then return to the squat. Repeat this exercise two or three times, as it is said that this action will open the ileocecal valve and help the drink stimulate your bowel. Do not be afraid to hold onto something so that you can negotiate the squatting exercise.

Next, use the neti pot as saltwater cleanse for the nose. Besides cleansing and stimulating the nasal mucosa, this prepares the nostrils for clear breathing during meditation, as it is preferable to breathe through the nose during meditation.

Setting the Spiritual Thermostat

Just as the morning thermostat is reset and the lights go on for the day's activities, so does our body/mind need to be reset for the purpose of the day. This means that I have to let go of the sleep mode and remind myself why I am alive in the world this morning. I call this process "setting my spiritual thermostat." I use one or more of the following techniques to do this.

Self-Talk Dialogue

Some days, I have a conversation between my adult and my inner child. I introduced this concept when we discussed the case example of Mr. and Mrs. Blue. Here, on my own, I take both roles, and I go back and forth expressing first one side and then the other. For example, this morning I may encourage my inner child to channel the fear of the new day into excitement about being alive. I want to let him know that I am there for him and will handle all the adult responsibilities that come up during the day. I have discovered that my own inner child has this particular fear that he has to handle the challenges of adulthood, and he feels overwhelmed by this task. I have counseled many patients who seem to have this same misunderstanding—that their inner child is responsible for all the "adult" challenges that occur during the day.

I introduce the idea that they have an inner psychological child and that they can relate to him or her and can visualize, talk to, comfort, and support him or her. This seems to bring almost instant comfort to the person with the realization that he or she does have an "adult" part that is perfectly capable of working in the world with all its difficulties and that the younger child within is not responsible for this and can relax and feel lighthearted and excited about life. Those of you who feel comfortable with this process, be sure to have the conversation be specific to your inner child's needs so that you have psychological balance right from the get-go in the morning. This method may take some time to practice, but you will be surprised how quickly you will be able to make good contact with your inner boy or girl and how peaceful you will feel after the dialogue. (For more information or if you want help with this technique, you can reach us at the Center for Holistic Medicine in Illinois.)

Personal Journal

I may review my personal journal. I love to write down my favorite thoughts, feelings, expressions, opinions, reminders, suggestions, aphorisms, and pieces of philosophy that I read or people tell me or that come to me in meditation or from study. I collect them and put them into brief, succinct, and readable pages of the journal. When I read it in the morning before the day's activities, I feel grounded and reminded why I am here and what my purpose is. It's like a wake-up call. Like a spiritual tap in the face, I read it and go, "Yes, sir, that's why I'm alive."

For example, the first line in my daily journal states, "I am a soul in this body doing this day's work." There it is, right in front of me, reminding me that I am a spirit in this particular body. Now I feel a little lifted out of the sleepy, coarse physicality of the night. And I'm reminded that this day is an opportunity that never has been before and never will be again. Wow. That is special. Now I'm beginning to feel a little of the specialness that life has to offer me—after reading the first line of my journal! For those of you who like to write, begin a journal of your own with words that have real meaning to you so that when you read your journal, it can ground you, give you guidance, touch your soul, and speak to your heart.

Spiritual Contemplative Work

I need to collect, review, learn, and study traditions that the sages from the past have recommended to us to help us live our lives. It's easy to become confused from within by our own erroneous thoughts or confused from without, meaning the constant input from news and the popular commentators of our times. The world is full of well-meaning but not helpful advice, trends, and people. The sages have knowledge that transcends "what's in" at the time of a particular culture's mores, and I feel uplifted when I study their advice. Their words give me something to shoot for, a psychological stretch, a spiritual stretching before I actually get to the physical stretching we call hatha-yoga.

For example, this week I'm studying the suggestion that "acts of kindness" literally support the world's continued existence and are very important. So yesterday, when the man changed the glass in the window at work, I tried to make him feel appreciated. When driving my car, someone let me in, and I made sure to give him a big wave of thanks. Last week, I shoveled some snow so the elderly neighbor could get to her mailbox. I'm trying to internalize that these "acts of kindness" really matter, and the sages are suggesting that I do them until it becomes a habit. This is one example of building your personality in the direction that you want to go. Find spiritual reading that you trust and let the wisdom of the sages speak to you each morning and help you expand yourself and grow "with the arrows pointed up."

Stretching, Breathing, and Meditation

After working with my mind and orienting it toward the day's purpose, I now work with my body. I begin a series of slow, deliberate stretching postures I learned from hatha-yoga classes. I am consciously coordinating my breath as I go in and out of the postures. When I pay attention to my breathing, I usually don't overstretch and hurt myself. After some time, I feel somewhat loose, flexible, and energized, and I am now ready to "sit for meditation." That may sound a little silly, but some say the main reason to do hatha-yoga is to prepare oneself to be able to sit comfortably and still without fidgeting and basically "get the body out of the way" for an extended period of time.

That was impossible for me until I learned hatha-yoga. At this point, I sit still and use the premeditative breathing technique that emphasizes the awareness of the breath in the nostrils mentioned in chapter 12. This breathing quiets the fight-or-flight response and balances the left (lunar) and right (solar) energies so that a balanced breath takes place. When this happens, this allows for the middle path of energy heretofore referred to as *sushumna* to exist. I experience this as a calming and centering presence of mind. At this point, I begin the formal process of mantra meditation. I focus on one of the chakra points and listen to the sound (mantra) repeat itself over and over and attempt to derive the benefits from meditation that we discussed in chapter 19.

Personal Prayer

After meditating and experiencing stillness, I am ready to talk to my Creator. I rise up from the sitting posture and pray. Spiritual traditions teach specific liturgical prayers or encourage speaking from the heart in a personal way. The latter can take the form of a simple conversation in which the person expresses his or her thoughts, feelings, and concerns to a "greater" consciousness.

Some people are not comfortable with the idea of a Spirit or Creator, and I suggest they address their prayer "to whom it may concern." This title seems to relieve a pressure or expectation to "believe" in something greater yet at the same time allows for an intimate conversation involving opening, trusting, asking for help, and in general, a supplication process. Here is an opportunity to ask for help with accomplishing their plans, fulfilling their health or financial needs, answering difficult questions, renewing their trust, recentering their lives, or expressing their hopes and dreams for what is to happen on this new day. It is often within the context of a personal prayer that people choose to do their day review or express their gratitude as discussed above. As you can see, the ideal path is for you to mix and match whichever method works.

Exercise

After prayer, if I have time, I change into appropriate clothing for exercise. I have already worked with my body for flexibility and balance. I will schedule a weight-bearing session some time during the week. Now it's time for some aerobic activity in the morning before starting the day's work as was suggested to me many years ago.

Over the years, I have found this to be good advice for two reasons. First, it is invigorating and gets the energy going, and the rest of the day feels physically easier, especially if I'm going to sit for most of the day. My body feels "exercised," and then I am not fidgety but feel comfortable using my brain the rest of the day. I also know that the circadian rhythm of our adrenal glands drives our cortisol levels to their highest around eight in the morning, and this provides a measure of anti-inflammatory protection with a little bit of "steroid high" encouraging us to "get up and get going" in the morning, so exercise fits in perfectly at this time. Secondly, even with my best intentions, I have difficulty initiating exercise in the evening and find it harder to begin an aerobic exercise session, be it too dark, too cold, too late, or I'm too tired, etc. Remember the discussion about exercise in chapter 11. As little effort as walking can help decrease all-cause mortality rates. I will walk, bike, and sometimes skip if I need to feel more challenged. Remember to exercise with awareness as we discussed in chapter 11 so you don't hurt yourself, and it becomes a pleasant experience.

Live the Day with Purpose

Now comes the opportunity to use your commitment, skills, and focus to use the principles in this book. During the day, you eat, think, and act in a healthy body that supports your living. Your mind, characterized by peace of mind and clarity of consciousness, can focus on the day's challenges while fulfilling your particular purpose in life, i.e., your unique soul correction specific to you, all the while improving the world around us.

Meals

Try eating using the principles we discussed in chapters 7, 8, and 9 concerning healthy food choices, food consciousness, and Ayurvedic food guidance. It is important to think of the food as being transformed into energy for your body/mind to use during the day. Ideally, take the time to chew and breathe as you eat and enjoy your meals. Talking or listening to others excessively will make this difficult. The key is to use your creativity so that you can remain social if you want and still pay attention to your own eating process and thereby nourish yourself at the same time.

Take a Break

Ideally, I like to find a fixed time and place (such as in the office with the doors closed) to renew my energy and focus. This is the time for a brief relaxation, exercise, breathing practice, or meditation. I find it very helpful to use this time to be private and focus inward. After five to twenty minutes of focused breathing or relaxation, I feel I have calmed down the fight-or-flight response and have let go of thinking about the morning or afternoon's challenges. In the quietude of this space, I reclaim my centeredness and remember that my purpose is to uplift my surroundings and myself with proper thoughts, speech, and action. This remembering feels very pleasant and grounding. This break can be applied in midmorning, before lunch, at midafternoon, or at the end of the workday to create a distinction between work and home life.

Evening Life—Self-Nurturance/Intimacy

The evening is a delicious time for inward productivity. With the energy of the sun ebbing comes a sense of letting go of action that transforms the outer world and the need to turn inward. Think of self-nurturing activities such as gentle stretching, bathing, prayer, or a brief meditation. Take some time to spend with your family or reach out to a loving friend, do some writing, or read for pleasure or spiritual growth. Create an evening life for yourself to make a gentle transition into nightfall where we will focus on the day's residue, next-day planning, and gratitude.

Appendix 2

Three Cases

1. Mr. Brown–Hypertension

Mr. Brown was a fifty-five-year-old father of two who presented with a five-year history of high blood pressure and a slightly elevated cholesterol level. He had been concerned about side effects from his medication and did not want to begin yet another medication to bring down his cholesterol. He was beginning to feel tired and low in energy and had the unpleasant sensation that "something is not right." He knew that there must be something he could do to help himself, but he didn't know what that was. He asked, "Can you help me?"

What Do You Eat?

I began treatment by discussing his diet history. For breakfast, he ate rolls and drank coffee. He usually had a sandwich for lunch. Dinner consisted of meat and potatoes or pasta, salad, wine, and dessert. After a little more dietary history, I made the following recommendations.

Reduce coffee and refined sugar products such as white breads, refined pasta, and pastries. Add fiber by adding whole grains, apples, mangos, and legumes. These are foods that have a low glycemic index, thereby reducing the exposure to simple sugars. This has the effect of lowering inflammation in the body, which may help blood pressure and prevent the arteriosclerosis process from creating heart disease.

Secondly, replace unsaturated oils with healthy fats, such as olive or sesame oil or clarified butter or coconut oil. These oils are less susceptible to free-radical damage and are thereby more likely to protect your arteries rather than damage them.

Supplements Can Help

A good-quality multivitamin that contains vitamin A, vitamin C, vitamin E, magnesium, calcium, and vitamins B_1, B_2, B_6, and B_{12} may help. Additionally, CoQ10 and essential fatty acids such as flaxseed oil or fish oil help to lower blood pressure and protect the heart.

Botanical medications such as guggul resin, Hawthorn berry, or red-yeast rice can be natural alternatives to lower cholesterol if that is advisable.

Energy medicines such as homeopathic remedies and tissue salts are made from minerals and plants. They are inexpensive and safe and cause minimal side effects if used properly. They can be used to treat high blood pressure. I began by prescribing Magnesium phosphorica 6x, three tablets four times a day. This low-potency homeopathic remedy is actually called a "tissue salt" because it contains very small quantities of magnesium and phosphorus that has a rebalancing effect on smooth-muscle tissue throughout the body. I'm hoping that the smooth musculature surrounding his arteries and veins will relax. Their constriction can cause high blood pressure, and their relaxation can allow the arterial walls to relax, dilate a little, and lower blood pressure.

Exercise

There is a wonderful health-fitness study involving the treadmill assessment of fitness in men. It showed that men who avoided being sedentary and who performed a certain minimum of exercise, such as walking, markedly reduced their chances of dying when compared to men who were sedentary (see chapter 11). Surprisingly, just a little exercise such as walking got these results!

I said, "You do not have to go to a health club every day. You do not have to have a high level of fitness to extend life. You just have to do *something*." I showed him that study, and right there and then he committed to walking twenty minutes a day.

Self-Observation

To help round out his treatment plan, he needed to learn a new way to look at himself so that he could watch and monitor his own progress with a sense of curiosity and hope. To this effect, our treatment team taught him awareness exercises. We first taught him a progressive relaxation technique in which he learned to relax his entire body. He was taught to relax the top of his head, then his facial muscles, then his neck, and continue progressing downward through the whole body to the toes. Can you picture the steps in the technique? At a later date and after some mastery with that technique, we then proceeded to teach him one of the breathing methods discussed earlier.

Both the relaxation and breathing practices helped him accomplish the two important life skills of focusing his mind and calming his nervous system *at will.*

Open Your Heart

At this point he was encouraged to talk with his wife or friends about his feelings and "open his heart." The idea is that we do not want him to "internalize" negative emotions and allow the stress to become embedded into his heart and blood vessels. What about people who have a difficult time talking about their feelings to others? Keep a writing journal and see how that works. They are told to write five minutes a day on the particular topic that is causing the stress. Oftentimes, patients will agree that they need to "talk it out" but feel uncomfortable. They agree to a writing journal. The next time I see them, I ask them to share their journal with me. Invariably, their journaling allowed for an opening within them. As they sit in front of me and read their journal, I find them more willing to discuss the matter outright—always with a sense of discovery and relief.

Find Your Purpose

I always ask a patient about his or her personal relationships and job life. I was taught that each one of us is here to fulfill a specific destiny. In most cases, a patient will tell me right off whether he or she is "on purpose" with his or her life. Almost all my patients agree that if they are not doing the right thing for their lives, they can see how their health would be negatively affected. I asked Mr. Brown two questions: Was he fulfilling his purpose in life through his work and family? Was he reaching for his potential and unique purpose for which he was created?

A Turnaround

What follows is an experience that I am fortunate to see often in my practice. When a person's "light bulb" gets turned on and he or she realizes that he or she can realistically affect his or her health in a positive way, it becomes fun to watch him or her as he or she learns, grows, feels empowered, and becomes happier in the process.

Here is what happened next as Mr. Brown took the recommendations to heart. He began to change things—slowly, at first; a little dietary change here, a little exercise there. He noticed that his energy picked up right after beginning the supplements. He practiced the breathing and relaxation techniques he was taught and used them at work and began to feel a sense of empowerment. His family noticed an increased sense of relaxation about him. He seemed more fun to be with. His blood pressure began dropping slowly and steadily into the normal range, and on one return visit he came in and said, "I've stopped my medication!" As time went on, he became more proactive, and he created his own plan for diet, exercise, stress reduction, and family intimacy. On another visit he announced, "I feel at home in my body and at peace with my life again."

Patient to Student to Teacher

Mr. Brown had succeeded in using his symptoms of hypertension as a means to learn about himself and grow as a person. He made the transition from a patient on medication, feeling somewhat helpless to help himself, to a student of his own health. The more he learned, the more confidence he gained, while radiating a sense of health and becoming an example for others to follow. At this stage of his health care, I think of him as taking the role of teacher. This often happens in the practice of holistic medicine. In the beginning, a person presents with symptoms and asks for help. In time and with effort, they transform themselves from patient to student to teacher!

2. Aaron—Laryngotracheobronchitis (Croup)

Aaron, age eighteen months, was lying on the floor coughing. The sound of the cough had a barking quality, and I could easily hear his labored breathing across the room. "Oh, oh," I wondered. Could this mean croup?

Reliving My Old Trauma

Croup is an illness associated with a virus that affects the airway. In some cases, the breathing passage is obstructed, which becomes a medical emergency. I became especially frightened not only because he was my son, but also because this brought up an old memory.

I was about twelve years old when I first heard the sounds of croup. My younger brother slept in the next room, and one evening, there were strange choking noises coming from his room. My parents were downstairs with some friends, so I got up to investigate and found him asleep, lying on his back, and struggling to breathe. I suddenly became scared. I ran to tell my parents. Before I knew it, they were on the phone with our pediatrician, who said, "Bring him into the emergency room."

I remember the frightening, worried sounds of my mother as they whisked him off to Michael Reese Hospital to have an emergency tracheostomy—a procedure in which a cut is made directly into the neck to open up a hole in the trachea (windpipe) to allow air to flow in and out of the lungs. The procedure was successful, and I believed they saved his life.

That was then. Now as I looked at my son, I felt the personal trauma of those memories repeating itself all over again. What should I do?

Homeopathy to the Rescue

I did two things. First, I called a physician who made house calls to come to the house and look at him because I wanted a second opinion. Next, I ran to the homeopathic remedy kit and took out the remedy Spongia (see chapter 13.) This remedy is indicated for a croupy cough that sounds like the bark of a seal. That is exactly what Aaron sounded like as he was lying on the floor struggling for breath with *inspiratory stridor*, a high-pitched crowing sound resulting from air trying to pass through the obstructed windpipe. I gave him one dose of Spongia and waited to see what would happen as I called my wife to sit by my side to steady my nerves.

What follows next is nothing short of a miracle. In about five minutes, he sat up and began playing with his toys!

I turned toward my wife and said, "Do you see what I see?"

There he sat, playing with toys even though we could hear that terrible wretched sound associated with someone trying to breathe through an obstruction in the throat. Ten minutes later, he was still playing.

One hour later, the doctor arrived, examined him, and said, "Croup."

I said, "Does he need to go to the hospital?"

He said, "I don't think so. When I listen to his chest, I hear that he's moving air in his lungs. His energy seems good. Let's watch him and see what happens." We watched as he played for a long while.

Slowly and steadily, his cough improved, his breathing improved, and so did my own experience of my personal trauma around the memories of my brother. One dose of Spongia, made from the sea sponge, cured both my son's croup and helped me heal from discovering my brother near death. Thank you, G-d, and thank you, homeopathy.

3. Arthritis and Depression, but Where Is Betty?

Multiple Problems

"I feel safe here," said Betty, as she began to cry softly. The pain of arthritis in multiple sites along with her other medical issues of hypercholesterolemia (too much cholesterol in the blood), hypothyroid (too little thyroid hormone production), high blood pressure, and depression had overwhelmed her. She felt that her health was going in the wrong direction. In our clinic, we often see people who become tired and frustrated after taking many medications. Oftentimes, their symptoms may have improved, yet they feel an overall loss of vitality. Over a period of time, they may become discouraged, if not outright depressed. I knew that following heart disease, stroke, and cancer, prescription medications were actually the fourth leading cause of death. I have spent many years as a physician working with people and their ailments and offering them natural solutions. Oftentimes, with G-d's help, we are successful. Yet something different was unfolding here. She was talking about feeling safe.

The Whole Person

"I've had trouble in other offices. They are all good people and mean well, but they focus on the part of me that is their specialty, and

I...I mean the me that is inside this body feels lost in the process." She again began crying softly. As I sat back in my chair listening, I remembered my experiences in medical school and afterward, where we were taught to treat a person as parts of a whole without the maturity or instruction to see that person and his or her symptoms, emotions, and lifestyle integrated into the beauty of a unique human being.

I had to go outside the mainstream and apprentice to various teachers and traditions to learn nutrition, supplementation, energy medicine (homeopathy), yoga and stress-reduction techniques, psychotherapy (including a spiritual perspective), and meditation. It took years for all this information to gel together into a working, practical, and curative way of practicing medicine so that I felt whole, complete, privileged, and blessed as a doctor.

Betty gently dabbed a tissue to her eyes, and her lips stopped quivering. As she was getting ready to continue, I realized that sitting here with her, practicing medicine this way, having like-minded practitioners around me, and working with our bodies, minds, and spirits on a daily basis, I felt safe as well.

About the Center for Holistic Medicine in Illinois

The Center for Holistic Medicine was founded by Dr. Rudolph Ballentine in Glenview, Illinois, on the grounds of the Himalayan Institute and was a fully functioning holistic medical clinic by 1978. In 1983, Dr. Gore began his apprenticeship/practice there and in 1997 moved the practice to a freestanding building designed and built for the purpose of practicing holistic medicine in Riverwoods/Deerfield, Illinois. During this time, Dr. Gore and his wife, Carol, added many practitioners to the staff in an organic way.

The vision of the center is to treat patients' symptoms, educate and empower them about their health, and help them grow as human beings. We accomplish this by treating the physical, energetic, mental, and spiritual parts of the patient. In order to accomplish this goal, we need a treatment team that covers all these areas of intervention. Currently, our staff offers services in holistic general medicine, family medicine, internal medicine, osteopathic medicine, functional medicine, chiropractic medicine, and holistic psychiatry. We also have doctors trained in naprapathy and naturopathy on staff. Other disciplines include nutrition, myofascial release therapy, acupuncture, homeopathy, biofeedback, psychotherapy, energy therapy (TAT® and

EFA), mindfulness sessions, stress-reduction lessons, and art therapy. We offer community lectures as well as in-house lectures and classes. These are announced online on our website and our Facebook page as well as in our newsletters.

Please feel free to contact us to receive our newsletter, to join our Facebook page, or to request more information about our services.

It is our privilege to serve you.

Jerry Gore, MD
Center for Holistic Medicine LLC Illinois
240 Saunders Road
Riverwoods, IL 60015
847-236-1701
E-mail: info@holistic-medicine.com
Website: holistic-medicine.com
Facebook: Center for Holistic Medicine Riverwoods Illinois

REFERENCE LIST

1. http://www.nytimes.com/2012/10/27/business/us-cuts-estimate-of-sugar-intake-of-typical-american.html.

2. Sanchez, Albert, et al. November 1973. "Role of Sugars in Human Neutrophilic Phagocytosis 1,2." *Am J Clin Nutr*: 1180–84.
   http://ajcn.nutrition.org/content/26/11/1180.abstract.

3. Tsugane S, Inoue M. 2010 May
   Insulin resistance and cancer: epidemiological evidence
   Cancer Sci.; 101(5): 1073-9. doi: 10.1111/j.1349-7006.2010.01521.x. Epub 2010 Feb 3. Review.

4. Mavrogiannaki, A. N., and I. N. Migdalis. 2013. "Nonalcoholic Fatty Liver Disease, Diabetes Mellitus and Cardiovascular Disease: Newer Data." International Journal of Endocrinology.
   Volume 2013 (2013), Article ID 450639, 8 pages
   http://www.hindawi.com/journals/ije/2013/450639/
   http://dx.doi.org/10.1155/2013/450639
   Review Article
   Nonalcoholic Fatty Liver Disease, Diabetes Mellitus and Cardiovascular Disease: Newer Data
   A. N. Mavrogiannaki and I. N. Migdalis
   2nd Medical Department and Diabetes Center, NIMTS Hospital, 12 Monis Petraki, 11521 Athens, Greece
   Received 9 March 2013; Accepted 12 March 2013

5. Groves, Barry. 2007. *Natural Health and Weight Loss. London:* Hammersmith Press. LTD. Appendix E page 308.

6. Cousens, Gabriel MD. 2003. "Raw Nut Bread," in *Rainbow Green Live-Food Cuisine.* Berkeley: Patagonia: North Atlantic Books. (We have used pizza crust numbers one and two and find it delicious and satisfying. 185-186.)

7. Cousens, Gabriel MD. 1992. *Conscious Eating,* Santa Rosa: Vision Books International.

8. Fallon, Sally, with Mary G. Enig. 2001. *Nourishing Traditions.* Washington: New Trends Publishing Inc.

9. Murray, Michael T., and Joseph Pizzorno. 2012. *The Encyclopedia of Natural Medicine.* New York: Atria Books. 726.

10. http://water.epa.gov/scitech/swguidance/fishshellfish/outreach/advice_index.cfm.

11. Van den Brandt, Piet A., and Leo J. Schouten. June 2015. "Relationship of Tree Nut, Peanut and Peanut Butter Intake with Total and Cause-Specific Mortality: A Cohort Study and Meta-Analysis." *International Journal of Epidemiology.*
    http://ije.oxfordjournals.org/content/early/2015/05/26/ije.dyv039.abstract?sid=f2d76e3e-10b7-4d68-b39a-466260e0cbae.

12. Fife, Bruce. 2005. *Eat Fat, Look Thin.* Colorado Springs: Piccadilly Books, 48–50.

13. Enig, Mary, and Sally Fallon. 2006. *Eat Fat, Lose Fat.* New York: Plume Books, 28–29.

14. Forette, B. et al. 1989. "Cholesterol as Risk Factor for Mortality in Elderly Women." *Lancet* 1 (8643): 868–70. http://www.ncbi.nlm.nih.gov/pubmed/2564950ruce.

15. Fife, Bruce. 2005. *Eat Fat, Look Thin*. Colorado Springs: Piccadilly Books, 58–63.

16. Ibid., 71. Cites Ravnskou, U. 1998. "The Questionable Role of Saturated and Polyunsaturated Fatty Acids in Cardiovascular Disease." *Journal of Clinical Epidemiology* 51 (6): 443–60.

17. Groves, Barry. 2007. *Natural Health and Weight Loss*. London: Hammersmith Press, 241. Cites Bang, H.O., et al. 1971. "Plasma Lipid and Lipoprotein Pattern in Greenlandic West Coast Eskimos." *Lancet* I: 11–46; and Feldman, S.A., et al. 1972. "Lipid and Cholesterol Metabolism in Alaskan Arctic Eskimos." *Archives of Pathology & Laboratory Medicine* 94: 42–58.

18. Sears, Barry. 2005. *The Anti-Inflammation Zone*. New York: Collins. (He discusses the value of the triglyceride/HDL ratio on pages 41–43.)

19. Fife, Bruce. 2005. *Eat Fat, Look Thin*. Colorado Springs: Piccadilly Books, 73, for a discussion about cancer and saturated fats.

20. Ibid. 73–74.

21. Ibid. 32, for a helpful table concerning percentages of saturation for different oils.

22. Enig, Mary, and Sally Fallon. 2006. *Eat Fat, Lose Fat*. New York: Plume Books, 61–62.

23. http://www.coconutresearchcenter.org/books.htm.

24. http://www.coconutketones.com.

25. As quoted in the *New York Times*: http://partners.nytimes.com/library/national/science/menshealth/archive/980113_963.html. Original study: http://archinte.jamanetwork.com/article.aspx?articleid=190898.

26. Sears, Barry. 2005. *The Anti-Inflammation Zone*. New York: Collins. (He discusses arachidonic acid beginning on page 22 and then throughout the book.)

27. Enig, Mary, and Sally Fallon. 2006. *Eat Fat, Lose Fat*. New York: Plume Books, 50–51.

28. Kay, Ruth M., and A. Stewart Truswell. 1977. "Effect of Citrus Pectin on Blood Lipids and Fecal Steroid Excretion in Man." *American Journal of Clinical Nutrition* 30: 171–175.

29. Brownstein, David. 2006. *Salt Your Way to Health*, West Bloomfield: Medical Alternatives Press.

30. Batmanghelidj, G. 1997. *Your Body's Many Cries for Water*. Vienna: Global Health Solutions Inc.

31. Lad, Vasant. 1985. *Ayurveda: The Science of Self-Healing.* Twin Lakes: Lotus Press.

32. Ballentine, Rudolph. 2007. *Diet and Nutrition.* Honesdale: Himalayan Institute Press.

33. World Health Organization. "Essential Medicine and Health Products Portal: The Role of Herbal Medicine." http://apps.who.int/medicinedocs/en/d/Jh2945e/2.1.html.

34. Kasilo, O. M. J., et al. 2010. "An Overview of the Traditional Situation in the African Region." World Health Organization's *African Health Monitor* 14: 7–15.

35. Fritts M, et al. 2008. "Traditional Indian Medicine and Homeopathy for HIV/AIDS: A Review of the Literature." *Res Ther* 5: 25. http://www.ncbi.nlm.nih.gov/pmc/articles/PMC2637286/AIDS.

36. For a more complete report, see Blair, Steven. 1989. "Physical Fitness and All-Cause Mortality: A Prospective Study of Healthy Men and Women." *JAMA* 262 (17).

37. Hilts, Philip. 1989. "Exercise and Longevity: A Little Goes a Long Way." *New York Times.*
http://www.nytimes.com/1989/11/03/us/exercise-and-longevity-a-little-goes-a-long-way.html.

38. Thune, Inger, et al. 1997. "Physical Activity and the Risk of Breast Cancer." *New England Journal of Medicine* 336: 1269–75. http://www.nejm.org/doi/full/10.1056/NEJM199705013361801.

39. http://www.repertory.org/d/node/202.

40. Kaminski, Patricia and Katz, Richard. 1994. *Flower Essence Repertory: A Comprehensive Guide to North American and English Flower Essences for Emotional and Spiritual Well-Being.* Nevada City: Flower Essence Society.

41. Akirav, Irit, and Mouna Maroun. 2007. Abstract. "The Role of the Medial Prefrontal Cortex-Amygdala Circuit in Stress Effects on the Extinction of Fear." *Neural Plasticity*, volume 2007. # 5. Extinction of fear: Interplay for dominance between the amygdala and the prefrontal cortex.

Made in the USA
San Bernardino, CA
02 June 2016